Reminiscences, Sporting And Otherwise: Of Early Days In Rockford, Illinois

John Henry Thurston

In the interest of creating a more extensive selection of rare historical book reprints, we have chosen to reproduce this title even though it may possibly have occasional imperfections such as missing and blurred pages, missing text, poor pictures, markings, dark backgrounds and other reproduction issues beyond our control. Because this work is culturally important, we have made it available as a part of our commitment to protecting, preserving and promoting the world's literature. Thank you for your understanding.

REMINISCENCES,

SPORTING AND OTHERWISE,

OF

Early Days in Rockford, Ill.

BY JOHN H. THURSTON.

ROCKFORD, ILL.:
PRESS OF THE DAILY REPUBLICAN.
1891.

Entered according to act of Congress, in the year 1891,
By JOHN H. THURSTON,
in the office of the Librarian of Congress, at Washington, D. C.

ROCK FORD.

Doct. Josiah C. Goodhue, the subject of this sketch, of whom a more extended notice is given in the body of this work, and author of the name ROCK FORD, was born at Putney, Vermont in 1803; graduated at Yale Medical College and commenced the practice of his profession at St. Thomas, Upper Canada, in 1824, where he was married to Catherine Dunn. He migrated to Chicago in 1832, and was prominent in the affairs of that city until he came to Rockford to reside in 1838. Doct. Goodhue was one of the founders of what afterwards became Rush Medical College at Chicago, and was elected alderman of the first ward at the first election under city organization in March 1837. His daughter, Mrs. C. F. Holland, now of Cedar Rapids, Iowa, who has heard him relate the incident of naming the town, supplies me with these facts.

During the summer of 1835, Daniel S. Haight and Germanicus Kent, then residing at what is now Rockford, William H. Gilman of Belvidere, John P. Chapin and Ebenezer Peck of Chicago, and Stephen Edgel, afterwards of St. Louis, met at the office of Doct. Goodhue on Lake street in Chicago, to name the claim, or mill privilege, which they hoped would at some time in the future become a town. All these were interested in the claim, as was Luther O. Crocker, for many years after a citizen of Freeport, Illinois. Mrs. Kent had suggested "*Midway*" as an appropriate title, it being nearly equidistant from Chicago and Galena, which name none of the interested parties approved. Various names were suggested and rejected, until Doct. Goodhue said "Why not call it ROCK FORD, from the splendid rock-bottom ford on the river there?" It seemed an inspiration, and was adopted unanimously.

CHAPTER I.

Introductory—The Team—Personnel of the Party—Good-Bye in front of the Troy House—Off for the Mississippi—The Route to Chicago—Arrival at Chicago—Make the Acquaintance of Long John Wentworth—Two Additional Members Join the Party—Meet D. S. Haight and B. T. Lee—Ride an Indian Pony to Rockford—Swim the Kishwaukee—Simeon P. and Mrs. Doty—Big Thunder—Arrival at Rockford—The Landscape Surrounding the Hamlet in 1837—Location of each Cabin in the Place—Haight's Log Cabin—Mrs. Haight the first White Woman in the Town—Her Remarkable Nerve—First Frame Building—Haight's Barn—The Barn used for Sabbath Services—Haight's Field—Prices for Seed Grain—The Race Track—Water for Domestic Use—Snakes—Cooking Range—Pioneer Bedsteads—Hoosiers from the Wabash—Hoosier Bacon—The Wabash Hog — First Bacon and its Flavor — Enterprising Hoosiers — Their Dress — Traveling Equipment — Harvest in 1837 — The Blackbirds — Seventeen Year Locusts.

At various times during the last thirty-five years, partial friends have urged me to write for publication the recollections of my boyhood days which were passed in Rockford. And more recently my young friends with sporting proclivities desire to see in type some account of the exploits of the Rockford boys with like tastes, who were here forty to fifty years ago.

An active boy of thirteen years, coming from an eastern city to a frontier settlement, would receive and retain impressions of scenes and events which fade from the memory of older persons. And further, what may be transpiring in the daily life of the inhabitants of a hamlet such as this was when I arrived, which this boy does not see or learn about, is scarcely worth looking after. The subject appears illimitable to my mind, and I cannot hope to do it justice. Only those who have tried it can realize how difficult it may be to accurately fix the dates and details of events which happened fifty and more years ago, particularly where one has memory only to rely upon. It is my intention to write mainly of the first doings and events which came under my observation previous to the period when there was a printed account made at the time; in many instances, they are such as a boy would remember most vividly, for the reason that the country, the people, their speech, and their manner of life, were entirely different from my previous experience. If, when Rockford shall celebrate its centennial in 1934, these reminiscences may serve to identify the time of events and the locality of objects, my purpose will have been partly accomplished, and I assure the orator of the day that I have made earnest efforts to write correctly. Hoping the reader may be a kindly critic of my crude composition, I commence the narrative by designating the route of a trip in winter nearly fifty-four years ago, from the Hudson to the Valley of the Rock river.

At about two o'clock in the afternoon of the first day of February, 1837, a pair of bay Morgan horses, bobbed, as was the style at the time, of unusual large size for that breed, were standing hitched to a sleigh in front of the Troy House, on River street, at Troy, N. Y. The team had been selected from the livery stock of "Ike" Van Ornum, in the rear of the hotel. Seated in the sleigh were Henry S. Osborne, of New York, William P. Dennis, of Massachusetts, Henry Thurston, of Lancaster, Mass., and the writer (born at Glens Falls, N. Y.,) of these reminiscences, then a lad of thirteen years. Grouped about the vehicle and on the sidewalk, were at least a hundred of the hotel, stage, livery, steamboat, and business men of the city. Some hot punch, brought out for the occupants of the sleigh, was duly imbibed, and my father gathered up the reins. "Git up Rob, g'lang Tanner," and amid a chorus of good-bye's and God bless you's, we were off for the Valley of the Mississippi. Ah! old Rob and Tanner, in your day the best coach team on the Troy and Albany turnpike, little did we know of the acres of mud and water through which we would wallow, the miles and miles of rolling, trackless prairie in Northern Illinois, without a vestige of the labor of man, over which we would roam during the next five years.

At Jamestown the sleigh was exchanged for a wagon, and we went on through Erie, Cleveland, Perrysburg, White Pigeon, Michigan City, to Chicago, where we arrived on the fourth day of March, and attracted by the sign on the building, put up at the New York house, on Lake street. My father, who was a hotel keeper, had for more than twenty years previous, followed that avocation at various localities on the Hudson, from Warrensburgh near its headwaters, to the city on the bay at the mouth of the stream, and possessing in an eminent degree the extensive acquaintance and bonhomie of the old time landlord, had found friends and acquaintances almost daily, from the commencement of the journey.

I was up betimes the morning after our arrival at Chicago, as it was my duty to see that the team was properly fed and groomed. Returning to the bar-room my attention was arrested by the appearance of a young man then in his twenty-second year, who was stalking about the room in his shirt sleeves, while holding an animated discussion with some of the bystanders. He was six feet 8½ inches in height; as straight as a gun barrel; had no visible beard; his hair of a light color, and looked as though he would weigh not to exceed 150 pounds. I was familiar with the streets of New York: could locate the country merchants who came to the city each spring and fall, and readily designate the nationality of foreigners who frequented the port, but here was an unique specimen of the "gentilhomme," the like of which I had never met, and I walked around him gazing at his surprising length with increased wonder at each revolution. With advancing years his frame filled out and he became round-shouldered, so that his great height was not so conspicuous, except when standing beside men of ordinary stature. There was a sink in one corner of the room, supplied with a tin wash-basin, a dipper and a bucket of water. Baring his neck and shoulders, he prepared to make his morning ablutions. As he stooped over, I moved up close behind him, and standing sideways took the measure of the inside seam of his trousers, the top end of which was the level of my shoulder, where I placed my hand, and stepping back, glanced back and forth from the floor to my hand, while mentally calculating the length of those legs. A burst of laughter from the bystanders caused "Long John Wentworth" to turn around, and then and there commenced an acquaintance which in later years ripened into a friendship only to be terminated by his death fifty-one years after. None of those who knew "Long John," by actual acquaintance or otherwise, will question his intellectual ability, but his personal appearance while a young man, before his frame had developed, was most remarkable. I can compare it to nothing more similar than a pair of tongs.

At Chicago, John Truly Shaler, of Lancaster, Mass., and John C. Kemble, of Troy, N. Y., who had made the journey by stage, joined our party. In Chicago we met Benjamin T. Lee, of Barre, Mass., and Daniel Shaw Haight, of Bolton, Warren county, N. Y., settlers at Rockford. Mr. Lee was an acquaintance of my father's, and Mr. Haight had known him in Warren county, N. Y., when he (Haight) was a boy, but for some reason did not make himself known until some months after. It was these two men who induced our party to locate in Rockford.

Mr. Haight was the first settler at Rockford on the east side of the river, early in the spring of 1835. He migrated from the town in the winter of 1847-8, and settled in Texas, near Shreeveport, La., and afterward, in 1853-6, paid brief visits to the city he founded. I have never been able to ascertain the date of his death, but it is a rumor that he was in the Confederate army and died since the war closed at Ft. Worth, Texas. Mr. Lee removed to Chicago early in the forties, and resided in that city until his death, April 25, 1879.

Mr. Lee traveled on horseback, and while in Chicago had purchased an Indian pony from Mark Beaubien, a noted character in the early history of Chicago, who "kept tavern like Sheol, and played the fiddle like the Devil," and who afterwards, in 1839-40, resided in Kishwaukee—"Rib Town"— at the mouth of that stream. Mounted on this pony and accompanied by Mr. Lee, I made the trip from Chicago to Rockford. We left Chicago on the afternoon of March

10th, via the Whisky Point road, crossing the Desplaines river at or near what was for many years after known as Spencer's tavern, this being the same place where the north road from Salt Creek to Chicago now (1890) crosses the river. The prairie for 12 miles out from Chicago was a sheet of ice. We made 18 miles the first day, staying over night at the Buckhorn tavern, a popular caravansary for a a generation afterwards. I do not remember where we crossed the Fox river, but it must have been some miles south of Elgin.

From Chicago to the Fox river the settlers' log cabins averaged about six miles apart. The evening of the second day we arrived at Pleasant Grove, two and one-half miles east of what is now Marengo, staying at the cabin of a Mr. Smith. There was but one inhabited house between Mr. Smith's and Fox river, a distance of about 25 miles. It was snowing in gusts the next morning, in places obliterating the faint trail. We rode through the grove and on the north side found a small cabin in which a man could not stand erect except in the centre, inhabited by three men, who instructed us to make for a point of timber six miles away, and on the opposite side of the prairie (Garden Prairie) where the trail was "blazed" through the timber to the ford at Kishwaukee river, at or near the present site of Big Thunder Mills, probably a mile east of Belvidere. The water was high and the ice had gone out in the center of the stream, while on both banks for some twenty feet in width it was strong enough to hold up a horse. On the west side a passage had been cut through the ice and there was a canoe lying on the east shore. We tried without success to drive the horses through the stream, intending to ferry ourselves with the canoe. Mr. Lee, an accomplished horseman, mounted his horse and forced him off the ice into the center of the torrent, only getting his feet wet in the passage. I mounted my horse and followed. When the pony struck the water he went out of sight, and I was wet to my shoulders. I afterwards passed this spot in company with Col. J. B. Beaubien, who said the Pottawattamie trail from Chicago to the lead mines crossed there. We made good time to Simeon P. Doty's, at Belvidere, and dried our clothes. I remember they gave me several doses of "blackstrap," (rum and molasses) then as now in good repute under like circumstances. We reached Rockford in the afternoon of the 12th of March.

Mrs. Doty acted as all good women would do in similar cases with a boy wet to his arm pits in ice water, whose mother was a thousand miles away. She stood me up before a blazing fire, turning me around from time to time, while Old Doty, on hospitable thoughts intent, stood by with his blackstrap to stimulate me. Mr. and Mrs. Doty were the first settlers in Boone county, in 1835.

Although not strictly germane to "Early Days in Rockford," some account of the burial place of the Pottawattamie chief, Big

Thunder, may be of interest. His last resting place was on the beautiful site now occupied by the court house in Belvidere, and was prepared in the Indian style. I first saw him in the summer of 1838. The body sat upon the ground facing south, and was surrounded by palisades about six feet high, except on the south, where they were lower, that he might see the whites when they came, and whom he predicted would come from that direction. The body was perfect when I saw it, with the exception of the head, which had been taken off by Dr. Josiah C. Goodhue, (who, by the way, always did do as the impulse prompted,) and carried away for some purpose of his own. It was surrounded by fragments of clothing, arms, etc. The ribs, legs and arms were in position, and portions of the flesh had dried, and were of the color of jerked meat. While they remained, the Indians made frequent contributions of ammunition, food and tobacco, which were placed in front of and within reach, for his use in the "happy hunting grounds." It is a legend that when Mr. Doty's supply of the weed ran short, he visited the Chief and borrowed the tobacco on hand.

In describing the town I shall have reference to the East Side of the river, unless otherwise specified.

The season of 1837 opened early, and as the earth became clothed in green it presented the most beautiful landscape I have ever seen. Innumerable flowers dotted the scene in every direction. What is now the second ward was covered with tall, thrifty white oak timber. The fires had killed most of the underbrush, and it was a magnificent park from Kishwaukee street west to the river, and from Walnut street south to the bluffs at Keith's creek. The trail to the ford wound through the south half of block 15, near Walnut street, down the hill in the rear of the high school building to the river bottom and entered the river where the present dam strikes the bank. On the opposite side, it left the stream nearly 200 feet below the dam. On the east bank below the ford was a high bluff, which at the time I write (1890) has been dug away at least 50 feet near the ford. This bluff was sodded to the water and crowned by a fringe of the largest red cedar trees in all the country hereabout.

Haight cut some of these trees in 1837 for posts to use in the fence around his dwelling on the corner of State and Madison streets. This fence, with the posts, afterwards fell into the possession of the late William Worthington, who sold it in 1882, and afterwards told his son the posts were as sound as the day they were put in. I am told some of these posts are now in possession of H. C. Scovill of this city, and are in sound condition.

Part of block 6, the whole of block 7, and the whole of block 17, now occupied by Thomas Scott's coal yard, and the Kenosha R. R. tracks, were covered with a dense thicket in which there was some large timber. I often killed partridges in this thicket, and once shot a wild turkey there.

When I arrived the town consisted of Daniel S. Haight's log cabin on the east end of lot 6, block 16, (north-east corner of State and Madison streets.) The frame of the main part of his dwelling house on the opposite end of the same lot. The frame of the main part of the Rockford House, on lot 5, block 7, (north-west corner of State and Madison streets,) Bundy & Goodhue's store (Harvey W. Bundy and George Goodhue,) on lot 1, block 8, (south-west corner of State and Madison,) fronting east. A log cabin built for Vance's store on the east end of lot 4, block 15 (on First street, opposite the hay market.) William Penfield's blacksmith shop, a frame building on lot 6, block 17 (corner Market and Madison streets.) Haight's barn, a large frame structure, near the square (north) at the intersection of State and Kishwaukee streets. A log cabin about ten rods south-east from this barn, occupied by a family named Kingsley. Mr. Kingsley was a carpenter who came from Belvidere, in 1836, to work for Haight on the Rockford House. Mr. William H. Tinker, now of St. Paul, Minn., writes me he boarded with him the winter of 1836-7. They used a cooking stove with one joint only of iron pipe, the balance of the smoke conveyor being of boards that took fire, and came near resulting in an autodafe. James Bosswell's cabin (he came from Huntsville, Alabama,) at or near the east end of lot 1, block 19, near Jonathan Peacock's premises. Jacob Posson's cabin in the locality of block 21, Gregory & Penfield's addition, and a small log hut which stood on State street, about 75 feet south-west from Haight's cabin and which he used for a stable. It was originally built for Bundy & Goodhue, and Mr. Goodhue told me he made $1,000 selling goods there. (?) These were all the structures within half a mile of the intersection of State and Madison streets, on the east side of the river.

Upon the west side of the river, my recollection is not so distinct. Germanicus Kent's cabin (he was the first to locate here in the fall of 1834, and came from Huntsville, Ala.,) stood about ten rods from the creek and eight rods east of Main street. His sawmill on the creek a short distance west of Main street. There was a log hut eight or ten rods below the mill that had been used for a blacksmith shop. Wm. E. Dunbar occupied a log cabin about one hundred yards south from the creek and twelve to fifteen rods east of Main street. Nathaniel Loomis and his son, Henry W. Loomis, (they came from New Jersey,) lived in a log house near the south-east corner of State and Main streets. Abiram Morgan's house stood on the present site of the Horseman homestead, the block bounded by Mulberry, North Winnebago, Peach and Court streets, and there was a cabin well up on the bank of the river about 130 rods from State street, occupied by Rev. John Morrill.

Haight's log cabin, the first structure on the East Side, was built early in the season of 1835 in regular pioneer style, without a nail, and a description will suffice for all such log houses. The body of the house, about eighteen feet square, was of oak logs with the bark on, the corners carried up by notch and saddle, the roof of shakes rived out from oak timber. The logs of the gable ends were fastened together with wooden pins. A pole is then laid lengthways of the structure two feet from the eaves, the shakes laid in two or more courses, and a pole put on top to hold them down. This process was repeated to the ridge pole. Short sticks were placed between the poles to keep them from sliding down. It had a puncheon floor, two windows, one door of puncheon stuff with wood hinges and latch, "the string on the outside." The cellar was simply a hole under the center. Haight had a cooking stove, but most of them had a fireplace at one end built of wood and outside; the fireplace of puncheons lined on the inside with clay and the chimney of split sticks laid up with mud. The spaces between the logs were chinked with wood and mud. Such a house may be built with an axe and an auger, and is a warm, comfortable dwelling. Haight made an addition in '36, with a space between ten feet wide and roofed over, which had a shingle roof and floor of sawed lumber.

Mrs. Mary Haight was the first white woman in Rockford, as Kent's family did not get here until two or three weeks after she came. She was a slim, alert, active woman, born and reared on the frontier, with no knowledge of books or literature, but possessed of good sound "horse sense," (I first heard this expression at that early day,) and of remarkable nerve, as two incidents which I had from her lips will confirm.

When they first came, they put up a tent under a large burr oak tree standing in State street near the site of the cabin. Shortly after, one night, Haight's cattle stampeded for their old home on Fox river and he started after them the next morning with no expectation of being away over night. He was gone five days and Mrs. Haight with her young child staid there without thought of fear or molestation from a camp of Indians near by. There were no whites within forty miles, except two of Kent's men on the West Side, and the Indian trader, Stephen Mack, at the mouth of the Pecatonica. She once left the family washing on the river bank while she went to the house, returning just in time to see a strapping Indian buck making off with the outfit. She followed him to the camp, half a mile up the river, went into the tepee and took the clothes away from him, the other Indians hooting in derision, "Squaw, squaw, squaw!"

Bundy & Goodhue's store was a one and a half story structure, of which most of the material was gotten out by hand; the studding, joists and rafters of small timber, hewed on two sides, and the siding and lath of split stuff. The floors and roof boards were of sawed lumber. This building is now standing, it being No. 211 East State street. Boswell's cabin was part logs and part split stuff. Possibly some among the few old timers who are still left, may remember "Mother Boswell's" potato pies. Were you there, Lish?

Haight's barn, built in 1836, was quite large, having a floor to thrash with three horses abreast. Thomas Lake and Sidney Twogood were the carpenters. They get all the material from the stump except the plank for the thrashing floor, and the boards to cover it. The timbers were massive, and it probably furnished the first "raising" in this county. Many years after, in talking with Mr. Lake of the event, he said it was a wonder where the people came from, as there was an abundance of help. The frame of this barn still exists on the farm of Isaac Rowley, near the city.

In the summer of 1837, this building was used for religious and other meetings. On the east and south sides it was surrounded by tall, thrifty white oak timber, with but little underbrush. A stand for the speaker was erected at one end, over the bay, the thrashing floor provided with seats made from slabs, and with the big doors open on a pleasant Sabbath day in summer, a more appropriate place for worship cannot be conceived.

Haight's field comprised a large portion of what is now the First ward. It was inclosed with a stake and rider worm fence. When I arrived, the corn he cultivated in '36 was standing in the field. All the grain he had was required for seed. He sold it—wheat, oats and corn—for two dollars per bushel, and could readily have obtained twice that sum. Richard Montague (on the West Side) had a few potatoes which he disposed of at $1.25 per bushel. The fence on the south side of this field commenced at the section corner near the foot of the hill on State street, and continued west on a straight line to the north-east corner of State and First streets, skirting the timber. This was the race track, and for a six hundred yards dash the start was near the section corner. Many and many a time have I been one of the jockeys over this course. Saturday afternoon was the regular race day, and the Hoosier horses were "right smart" for a quarter dash, the wagers ranging from drinks for the crowd to an old bull's eye watch. In fact, the first collection of people of which I have a recollection, was a foot race of one hundred yards between one of the Broadies and William Bundy, at which my father officiated as one of the judges at the start, and John C. Kemble at the finish.

Water for household use was hauled from the river in a cask fastened to the crotch of a tree; for drinking water a barrel was sunk in the river bank about one hundred feet above State street. There were some large springs gushing out of the bank on the west side, at the present site of the water works, and in summer I frequently went there in a canoe for a supply. A trail on each bank of the river extended as far as I explored, made by the Indians in their hunting, and in August the grass beside this trail would completely hide a man standing erect. Snakes were abundant. I once killed a massaugua (local name for rattlesnake) in the path to the water barrel. The hogs which ran loose soon made them scarce.

My father secured the Vance cabin for his family when they should arrive, and early in May he and I commenced house-keeping there, having for cooking utensils a frying pan and a large box stove. We afterwards secured an iron bake kettle, a most useful implement as I can testify, it being well adapted to bake, stew, fry, boil, washing dishes, and also available for toilet purposes in the early morning. A bedstead was constructed for my parents in a corner of the cabin, with one leg, the two rails being framed into the logs, and short boards laid across to support the bedtick filled with prairie hay. For the rest of the family hickory poles were used for bedsteads, an axe and an auger only being required for their construction. My brother and I went aloft on a ladder to our sleeping apartment next the shake roof, and when the first snow came one windy night, we woke up in the morning with two inches of snow on top of us.

Our only provisions came from Chicago, Ottawa (the nearest grist mill), Savannah and Galena. In the early summer, the "Hoosiers from the Wabash" made their appearance, with droves of cattle, horses, hogs, and "prairie schooners" loaded with bacon. This meat was most excellent as they kept it at home in the smoke house, but in hot weather, after a four weeks' journey in the "schooner," it became, had its population united their strength, capable of traveling alone. You may ask if I ate such stuff. Well, yes, I did. Most of them—part of them would crawl out, and they were dead anyhow when thoroughly fried.

The Wabash hog of 53 years ago has become extinct, even in his native haunts. Possibly he may still roam in some parts of Arkansas; to his credit be it said, he fulfilled his mission in life most admirably. His most striking points were head, ears, legs and tail, all of which were abnormally large in proportion to his body, which was fashioned after the pattern of a shingle and made most delicious bacon. With all, he had the speed of a quarter horse, as I soon ascertained when I tried to head him off while mounted on my pony. Late in the fall of '37, my father and Mr. Haight bought a drove of forty head, which were slaughtered on the spot now occupied by the engine house, corner of First and Walnut streets. A box was made for scalding and the water heated with hot stones. The meat was cured in bulk, and was the first put up for sale in the town. I may add here as a finish, that a little rust and some hair gave a flavor to the bacon which is now and will remain unknown to the present generation.

The Hoosiers of that day were an enterprising set of men, and in sharp business transactions could discount a Yankee from the Nutmeg state. Early in the summer they loaded their "schooners" with bacon, and with droves of stock migrated to northern Illinois, where they spent the season in breaking the prairie and selling their stock, camping out the entire time they were away from home. Retaining sufficient team for the "schooner," they returned via Chicago, where the vehicle was loaded with salt and they arrived home with the entire proceeds of the venture in cash.

Their dress was blue jeans, the cloth made at home, and occasionally some young fellow was quite stylish in a swallow tailed suit. These men were most accomplished horsemen, and when traveling light were always on horse back. Their equipment was light, simple and most admirable for the purpose. They wore spurs and leggins. For leggins about three-fourths of a yard of blue jeans was required for each leg, and a good deal of skill may be displayed in putting on and securing them. When unusual skill was shown in the outfit, indicating the rider "to the manor born," he was at once taken to be an itinerant preacher or a horse thief, with the chances in favor of the circuit rider.

The summer of 1837 was wet; the crop was superb. My father cultivated a part of Haight's field, the oats weighing 42 pounds to the measured bushel. At harvest time the blackbirds made sad havoc, alighting on the small grain in numbers sufficient to break it down. In some localities they tore open the husks on the ears of standing corn. I shot and gathered nearly half a bushel of them one afternoon, with which my mother made a splendid pot pie. To the consternation of the settlers, who anticipated disastrous results, the seventeen year locusts made their appearance in incredible numbers, and have returned regularly since that year, but not to such an extent in this vicinity.

CHAPTER II.

First Lawyer, his Wife and her Slave—The Millers—Washington House—First Frame Dwelling occupied by a Family—First Frame Dwelling in the County—Thomas Lake—Claim Fight—"Let's go and get a Drink"—Reminiscences of Thomas Lake—He Sails from England in 1832—Arrives at Cleveland—Pioneer Life in Ohio—Illinois Fever—Arrives at Chicago—Chicago in 1835—Ducks and Mud—Doctor Goodhue—Difficult to Secure Transportation—Starts for Rockford—In sight of Newberg—The Kishwaukee Impassable—Takes possession of an Empty Log Cabin—Stays there Two Weeks—Nearly Drowned in the Kishwaukee—Arrives at Rockford.

John C. Kemble, of our party, was the first lawyer in Rockford. He was a man of ability and had been a member of the New York State Legislature from Rensselaer county. He became insane, and in 1840 was taken to an eastern asylum, where he died soon after. His wife was a member of one of the old Dutch families of New York; as was the custom of that day and time, when she was born, a young slave belonging to the family was designated as her servant, whose special duty it should be to look after her personal welfare and comfort while he lived. This duty "Black Ike" (Isaac Wilson) fulfilled to the extent of his ability. Mrs. Kemble followed her husband to Rockford in the fall of 1837, and the following year "Black Ike," true to the devotion, traditions and customs of his race to the family of whom they were slaves, came to Rockford and resumed his duties as her servant.

The Kembles had two sons, both possessed of more than average ability. Albert, the eldest, became a painter and went to Italy to prosecute his studies; was married and died there. Edward had literary tastes and abilities of a high order. He edited and published a boy's newspaper in 1840, from the office of the *Rockford Star*, called *The Comet*. For the last forty-two years I had preserved the only copy of this paper known to be in existence, but when I came to look for it recently it was gone, cribbed, stolen. May perdition seize the thief! Edward went around the Horn to California with a printing outfit, and established the first English newspaper in San Francisco, *The California Star*, before that name was applied to the town. He was there when gold was first discovered in the state. During the late unpleasantness, he was a paymaster in the United States army. He died in New York City about four years ago, having for some years previous served as news agent for the California Press Association.

Jacob B. Miller, ("Old Jake") the second lawyer to locate in Rockford, was a most eloquent speaker, and in great demand by the whigs of this locality during the coon-skin and hard cider campaign of 1840. The Millers arrived about the middle of May, 1837, and were prominent in the affairs of the town while they remained. They built the Washington House in 1838, on the east end of the lot on the southeast corner of State and Madison streets. The father, John Miller, with a second wife and three grown sons, Jacob B., Thomas and George. Another son, Alexander, was here in the summer of 1838. The Millers arrived earlier than they were expected. They had an arrangement with Haight by which he was to vacate his log house for their use. Haight had a force of carpenters at work upon his dwelling house on the corner of State and Madison streets, who were set at erecting a small frame dwelling house on lot 9, block 16, and which he occupied as soon as it was inclosed. This was the first frame building occupied by a family in Rockford. The Millers had a small stock of merchandise which they opened in the carriage house attached to Haight's dwelling. They had two "prairie schooners" with ox teams that were kept at work all the summer hauling merchandise from Chicago and Savannah. Some years ago Mr. James B. Martyn, an Englishman, who came here from Huntsville, Ala., in 1836, at the solicitation of Germanicus Kent, told me he erected the first frame dwelling in 1836 in this county, on his claim on the State road, one mile east of the intersection of State and Kishwaukee streets.

Mr. John Lake, of this city, has kindly consented to the publication of the following document found among the papers of his deceased uncle, Thomas Lake, who came to Rockford in 1835. It does indeed give a most graphic account of the trials and hardships encountered by the pioneers of early days in Rockford, and in several instances confirms my own recollections, which were written before I knew of the existence of the paper. I, too, can confirm incidents therein mentioned, as I knew of the buckwheat being sown in the standing corn. I was present at the claim fight he describes, which came off some two miles northeast of the town, where Mr. Brown defended his castle, and saw the rifle barrel protruded between the logs. My father had given me strict orders to sit in the wagon right there where he left me, and hold Rob and Tanner, but the opportunity to see a fight with guns was too much for my boyish nature, and I hitched the team to a convenient sapling and stole up Indian fashion, from tree to tree, to the scene of the expected battle. Early one beautiful morning in August twenty-three ago, I was at Charles City, Iowa, and stepping out on the sidewalk, the first person I met was

"Jake" Waller, the pioneer who located on what is now part of the poor farm. "Jake," said I, as I shook his hand, "How do you do?" He looked at me long and earnestly, but memory gave him no recollection of the boy and the claim fight. "I don't know you." "Well, Jake, the first time I saw you, we were each behind a big tree as a breastwork to stop a stray bullet." "You are John Thurston, by ——, let's go and get a drink."

It will be noticed that Mr. Lake's reminiscences close quite abruptly, and I am inclined to think from a conversation I had with him some years ago, when I told him I had prepared a paper of the history of my family and my early life in Rockford, for the perusal of my children, that he had the same object in view.

REMINISCENCES.

Thomas Lake was born on the fourth day of July, 1806, at Blackford, in the parish of Selworth, county of Somerset, England, of parents named William and Elizabeth Lake. His father was a farmer, carrying on the milling business in connection therewith. The Lake homestead belonged to the estate of Sir T. D. Ackland.

His chief occupation, up to the time of his father's death, soon after which he sailed for the United States, was farming. Prior to this time he was married to Miss Lavina Atkins, daughter of Mr. John Atkins, a farmer living at Whitcomb, parish of Minehead; his mother was still living.

I sailed from Bristol in May, 1832, on board the bark Charlotte; the voyage was a tedious one of seven weeks and three days. We landed in New York at the breaking out of the cholera. There had been forty deaths on board a French vessel that spoke us at sea.

I had letters of introduction to parties in New York, but the city was terror stricken, and business at a standstill, and no hope of employment. We were advised to go on west; after remaining in New York a few days we concluded to do so. Arrived at Troy, I soon found employment, but this lasted only a short time, as thousands had left, and were daily leaving, on account of the cholera, which had already reached the city, and was rapidly spreading. There was nothing doing, and it would not do for us to be idle.

We had one child, born to us before we left England, Robert W. We concluded to go to Buffalo by canal; the trip occupied about two weeks. There was another family accompanying us—man, wife and one child. On our arrival at Buffalo, the first thing was to look for some respectable tavern to stop at; this we failed to find. Having come from Troy and New York, no one would take us in, where we could think ourselves safe until morning. Our families still remained on the boat. After looking around till tired out, and finding no hopes of quarters that looked safe, we concluded to go on to Cleveland. Having made up our minds, we took passage on a schooner; the weather was very rough, but the wind being in our favor, we made a quick voyage.

When within signaling distance, a flag was run up at the fort, ordering us to drop anchor. After continuing on our course for some distance further, a second flag was run up. The captain took the hint and dropped the anchor. We soon saw a boat put out from the harbor and make for the schooner. By this time the wind had abated enough to allow the boat to put alongside. Three gentlemen jumped aboard—doctors. We passed through a strict examination as to where we were from, where we had stopped by the way, whether the cholera had broken out at New York and Troy before we left, and where we were bound for. These questions were answered by the captain, and we tried to look our very best, having been warned as to the expected object of the visit. While the doctors were holding a council, the captain informed us that he probably would have to take us back to Buffalo, without landing his cargo.

I was standing alone, looking over the bow, when one of the doctors approached me with the question, "Will you tell me your wife's name before she was married?" I told him. "Had she a brother named Tom?" "Yes." "Was he educated at Oxford?" "Tom," he said, "was my school and room-mate, but he took to law and I to physic." After a few minutes talk alone with his associates, we were allowed to land; but people were afraid of us. We took the best quarters we could procure, and the bedbugs would have finished us had we not gotten up and dressed. We went out early to see to unloading our things, not knowing what to do or where to go—dismayed and disheartened at our sad lot. A farmer passing by, seeing our luggage piled up on the wharf, enquired where we were bound. He advised us to go into the country, where he lived; told us there was no hope for us where we were but to spend what we had.

So we started for Strongsville, a distance of fifteen miles. With much difficulty we rented part of a house occupied and owned by Moses Pomroy, a carpenter and joiner. I commenced mowing and haying for a man named Strong, who had been living here about twenty-five years, and had a large farm cleared off, and some good orchards. The heat, to me, was intolerable. I felt as though I should drop at my work, but I stuck it out as best I could till haying was over.

My next job was harvesting for a new man, on a ten acre lot, cleared off in the middle of the woods; heavy timber of a tremendously tall growth all around us. It came on from hot to hotter; I suffered dreadfully. I was binding after my employer; he was a powerful man, and had informed me that it was impossible for one man to keep up in binding after his cradle. I had striven hard to keep up, but the heat was too much; I dropped senseless to the ground. My employer at last saw me, and ran and picked me up, carrying me into the shade of a large tree; he administered some restoratives for sunstroke, and after awhile, he said, I began to kick; but I was very ill, being scarcely able to stand. His neighbors blamed him very much, as it had nearly cost me my life. I was both sick and weak for a long time, but continued to work, as it was necessary I should do what I could, as I had found that seventy-five cents a day did not bring in money very fast, and left almost nothing, after paying house rent, and buying fuel and provisions.

After harvest there was but little work in view. We were often asked to buy a farm. We found a great many wished to sell, as is the case in all new countries, and old, too, wherever I have been. We were well dressed—far different from our neighbors—and our clothes were scrutinized closely. People in this country dress very differently now to what they did in 1832. It was generally the rule then for people to live within their means. A farmer owning two or three hundred acres could be seen, of a Sabbath, with his wife behind him on horseback, riding off to meeting, with a child or two before him, if they were not old enough to walk the distance. Well, as we were well dressed, it was thought we must have lots of money; as it was always thought people coming from England had. Friends flocked around us; some wished to sell, some wanted to borrow. We never tried to convince any one whether we had much or little. "Did not know but that we should return in the spring," was our reply. This was as far down in the mystery as they were allowed to get; in truth, we had but little money. Our neighbors were very kind, as I believe is generally the case where the land is in the market.

About this time, winter began to look me sternly in the face. I was convinced that I could not clear heavy timber land at ten dollars per acre, which was the price then paid.

One Sunday, after meeting, I was returning with Mr. Pomroy. He was extolling the advantages of a good trade. He replied, "What will you give me to show you what I know, seeing you think so much of a trade?" "Me to give you," I said, "is out of the question; pray what will you give me at the bench for the next six months?" "Ten dollars per month," he replied; "but you will have to board yourself, pay me rent, find your own fire-wood, etc." "When shall I begin?" "To-morrow morning, if you wish."

In the morning, at sunrise, the shop was all cleaned out, and I waiting for orders. I was put to jacking down some boards to a thickness—not an easy task for a new beginner, but I got along pretty well, he said. A few days after he had a lot of window sash to make. I was to rip out the stuff and dress it up; he would put them together, he told me, and left after giving directions. I have seen sash stuff much better dressed, and I have seen much better sash, but they passed. There was always much doubt in my mind whether the stuff was not much better suited for kindling.

So we dodged along into winter. I soon found that the work was not so hard as at first, and I could dress up pieces of stuff that would go together better. We had some jobbing, alterations and repairs for our neighbors. He was drawing $1.25 per day when out of the shop, and work plenty. We always had our board when out. At or near spring, he took a job finishing off a tavern near Cleveland, and took me with him Monday mornings, returning Saturday nights.

One evening, after supper, I told Mr. Pomroy I believed my six months was out. "You ain't going to leave me, I hope?" "I can't support my family, you know, with but ten dollars a month." "How much do you want?" "Make me an offer so I can live, and I will work for you till this job is finished." He made me an offer, and I continued on till the job was completed. He then wished me to hire to him for the next twelve months. I told him I was going to Cleveland in a few days.

I arrived in Cleveland a total stranger. Looking around me, I saw men at work framing a large building. I watched them until I thought I knew who was the boss carpenter. I asked him if he wanted to hire more help. "Yes, what wages do you want?" He made me an offer of twenty-five dollars per month and board. I accepted, and told him my family was at Strongville. I told him I would be on hand on such a day, as I had no working clothes or tools, of which I had been buying a few. I continued with him the time agreed upon, and then quit. I had been cautioned to draw my pay as fast as I could, as my boss would soon break down, then I would lose it. The same man wanted to hire me when I left; he being a stranger, I thought perhaps this may be all gotten up. I had worked about two weeks; on Saturday I asked him for my money. He told me he could not give me any. Then I told him I must quit, as it was quite necessary my family should have something to eat, and that I should have to get my pay weekly. He paid me some, and I started for home—fifteen miles, a nice little walk,—after sunset and a hard day's work. I had to get back Monday morning soon enough to commence work. Our hours then were from sun to sun in the summer, and till nine by candle light if the building was enclosed or we were in the shop, in winter, except Saturdays. I used to work my six days and then walk thirty miles by way of change. I had tried to get a house, but had failed so far. My wife was comfortably situated where she was, and I hated to move her until I could do somewhere near as well. I at last succeeded in renting some upstairs rooms, and moved my family in; but when we lighted the fire we found the chimney was built the wrong end down—it was a smokehouse of the first order, and unbearable; so we had to do without fire, and try to cook below, until we could do better. After a little I heard of a house that was going to be vacated, but it was a larger house than we needed, and more rent than we could afford to pay. I was in hopes the owner would let me part of it; but no; he would let me all of it, and I could let part, only he should look to me for the rent. We rented it. Now we began to live again. As we had a large house, more room than we needed, we soon had applicants for board. My wife concluded to take three or four, but found it did not pay, as she could not afford to set as good a table as she thought she would be able to if she had a greater number. So we fitted up to accommodate ten or twelve—a greater number had applied than we could take. Now we found we could set a better table and make a profit. I continued to work as usual. We had as happy a lot of young men as I ever saw; all joiners but one—he was carrying on a shoe shop close by.

I became acquainted with a young Englishman, a shop mate. His father was taken ill, and sent for him. Told him he owned a quarter section of land in the vicinity of Beardstown, Ill., and if he would go and look it up, he would give it to him, if it was worth having. He found it to be valuable property, with a saw mill built on it. He was greatly pleased with the country, and spoke of those extensive prairies, where you could plow for miles without striking stump or stone. This gave me the "Illinois fever."

I had bought a piece of land, nine miles from Cleveland, on the state road to Columbus; but it was covered with a tremendous growth of timber except ten acres which I had hired cleared and fenced. I found I was a very poor hand with the ax; I worked one half day on it burning tree tops in July, and made a vow it should be my last. I had an opportunity to sell my interest; I had made some small payments as they came due. The lot was 120 acres owned in New York.

We had just began to lay up a little money, and my wife was opposed to breaking up house-keeping, as we then had become comfortably fixed. But I had left my home in England with a determination to own a farm, if my health and strength would serve me. So at last with sorrow to leave our friends, we set about preparing for our journey to Illinois. This was in September, 1835. We had a sale and sold off, or gave away, all our things that we did not wish to take with us; agreed for our passage on board the schooner Illinois, for Chicago. Having our things loaded upon the wagon, my wife and Robert in a buggy, our boarders—insisting that they would see us safely off—took the horses from the wagon and hauled our family and effects down alongside the schooner. The buggy I could not sell, except at too great a sacrifice, and I concluded to take it along. Our boarders took charge of our effects till they were safely stowed on board. All things now being ready, the schooner set sail. A fair wind soon wafted us out of sight of our true and dear friends, they still standing on the wharf, getting smaller and smaller, till lost in the distance. Then, with our faces turned toward the promised land, we had quite a pleasant time. The captain had agreed to board us, and deliver us and our effects for a certain sum. He proved to be a very good and kind man to us, and landed us in Chicago, October 1st, 1835.

Chicago, then and now, look very different; there was no shipping in the river. On our arrival, after making fast to a stump, a few visitors came on board, anxious to know about the staff of life— flour, pork and other eatables. As provisions were getting scarce, and many were out of these things, the vessel's small supply was soon disposed of at a big figure. We had, fortunately, laid in a supply of flour and pork, and a few other necessities, before we started, that would last us for some time. One of our visitors, named Steel—a hard name, but proving a very kind friend to us—wished to know if that was my tool chest standing on the deck. I told him it was. He wanted to know if I wanted to work, and if so, how soon would I be ready. I answered as soon as I could get a house, or room, for my family. I found this to be no easy task, but at last succeeded in getting shelter—it was useless to be particular in those days. The second or third day after, I commenced work for my new acquaintance, and continued to work for him till I started for Rockford, much against his advice, as he wished me to continue with him. Steel was elected and served as sheriff of Cook county after I left.

The houses then were few and far between. The walls of the Lake House were up when we arrived. I worked on it for a while, but most of my time was spent on a brick house Mr. Steel was building over on the South Branch, for a residence for himself.

There were two things very plentiful in and about the city, especially after a rain—ducks and mud; and as I had no desire to go into the duck trade, I concluded to seek a more solid foundation for the soles of my feet. Some time late in the fall I met an old acquaintance from Cleveland, a Mr. Twogood. Being out of a job, he joined me at the bench. Mr. Twogood and I were of the same opinion in regard to life in Chicago, and often talked of going out where we could get a farm. A compact was finally made to trust our fortunes together; as he had a wife and, I think, three children, it would be much pleasanter for both. So it was finally decided "whither thou goest, I go also."

About Christmas, my wife being sick, I called in Dr. Goodhue, then practicing in Chicago. I told him I did not intend to settle in Chicago, as my object in coming to this country was that I might own a farm. He insisted that I could do no better than to go to Rockford, and described the locality and its surrounding advantages, and stated that he had an interest in the town.

The greatest difficulty was in getting there. We found that we should be obliged to cross a number of streams—many of them quite large—and no bridges, except when frozen over. It had been quite cold, and those streams were now safe; but, as it was getting well along in February, a thaw might set in at any time, and compel us to wait until the ground became settled, which would be too late in the spring.

To hire teams for the journey was no small task. The rule with teamsters was to find out how much money a person had, and then, if possible, extort the last cent. After an agreement had been entered into, and signed, and everything under way, miles from any house, they would threaten to go no further unless you gave an embargo on all your effects. Fortunately we entered into a written contract; a portion paid in advance, and the balance when our goods were delivered safely in Rockford. As they were boarding at our expense, they were in no hurry to start mornings, and were only too willing to stop at night, if shelter and accommodations could be found, so we made but poor progress. The weather became warmer after we started, and the ice soon weakened. As we were crossing Fox river, one of our wagons broke through. We had to unload and fish out our things as best we could. After much labor we got our goods on the other side and loaded up, hoping to get a good start in the morning. But next morning we found a mutiny had broken out amongst our teamsters, and they refused to go any further. We agreed to leave the matter to our landlord, and abide by his decision. The contract was produced, and he told them they had better go on, as their pay was ample, if not extravagant.

After much delay we were under way again, but the teamsters were sulky, and our progress was slower, if possible, than it had been. Thawing continued. After many delays—wagons breaking down, sometimes going through the ice, harness giving out—we at last arrived, tired and weary, in sight of Newburg. The flat was under water, and the ice in the river broken up and going down stream at a terrific rate. The teams were stopped. With great difficulty some of us got near enough to converse with the people on the other side. They told us it was useless to think of crossing, and that, possibly, the water would not subside for two or three weeks. Our only course was to submit to circumstances that were entirely beyond our control. We had been informed that there was an empty log house somewhere up the river, toward Belvidere. Sick at heart, worn out and disgusted, we started on the search. About two miles west of Belvidere, in the edge of a grove, we found the cabin. We took possession in the name of "Necessity," and unloaded our things, making ourselves comfortable for the night—some cooking, others nailing quilts around the sides, to prevent ourselves from being blown through the cracks. It was not much of a palace, as it was only put up to hold a claim till some customer came along, or some friend came out from the east, or perhaps it was made for some prospective baby—these claims were many and quite extensive in those days. We had no trouble with the owner, as the place was for sale, and we convinced him that we did not intend to take permanent possession, but would move off as soon as we could cross the Kishwaukee, and also that we were willing to pay him for the shelter it afforded us.

Our teamsters, when viewing their situation, seeing that they would not be able to fill their contract for two or three weeks, knowing and being told that they had wasted two or three days on the road and should have been at their journey's end before the ice went out, were changed men. After a good supper, we fixed up as comfortable as possible, and retired for the night, and perhaps some slept soundly—but not all. The first to be attended to in the morning was breakfast, after which we settled with our teamsters. They had calmed down considerably from the high position they held a few days before; but everything was satisfactorily settled and we parted in the best of fellowship.

It kept Mr. Twogood and myself busy all that day fixing up to make the place comfortable. Then we began to think of Rockford. One man had to stay with our families, we could not leave them alone for fear of the Indians; so the matter was settled by lot, and fell to me. It was with considerable difficulty that I got ferried over the Kishwaukee—this was in March, 1836—and started for Rockford.

I was kindly received by Daniel S. Haight and wife. They had a double log house, but only half of it finished. The other half had only the roof on, made of four feet shakes—neither floor nor windows, but sufficiently light and airy. I told him our situation, and he offered us the unfinished part if we could fix it up so as to be habitable, till we could do better. After partaking of a hearty meal with him and his kind wife, I made the best of my walk back. Perhaps it was the next day, Mr. Twogood visited Rockford, and received the same kindnesses as myself. We concluded to accept Mr. Haight's kind offer as soon as possible.

We were compelled to stay in our present location for nearly two weeks. Getting tired of our constant trips to Rockford, and having but little hopes of the Kishwaukee becoming low enough to ford, we made arrangements with Mr. Haight to meet us at Griggsville (now Cherry Valley.) We were to have our things moved as near as possible on the opposite side. There being two canoes there, we lashed them together and ferried our goods across, a few at a time.

We got our families over first and started them for Rockford, where they were kindly received by Mrs. Haight.

Mr. Twogood was a steersman, I working forward. The stream was very rough, and our impromptu ferry not too easily handled. About midstream we struck a snag, and in trying to save something from being lost in the river, I went overboard. I should probably have been drowned but for Mr. Twogood; he caught me as I was coming up the second time. We got ashore as quickly as possible. All of our clothes had gone on the trip with our families, so I had nothing to do but reach Rockford as best I could. My clothes were freezing stiff, and chafing me badly. When I got through the timber I discovered smoke coming from a new cabin, raised the day previous. I took heart and hurried on, with difficulty reaching it. There was a roaring good fire burning, but as soon as I felt the heat, I began to feel sick and dizzy, and darkness surrounded me. Mr. Smith, the owner of the cabin, came to my rescue with a little cordial, left after the raising. After getting thawed out and a little rested, we started on. Arriving at Rockford we found our families enjoying the kind care of Mrs. Haight. I felt next day as though I had been not only scalped, but skinned. Mr. Twogood and I, with the assistance of our better halves, busied ourselves fitting up the inner walls of our new quarters with blankets, sheets, quilts, etc., so that it was comfortable for the night.

After we had rested and looked around for a day or two, Mr. Haight made an arrangement to have Mr. Twogood go on and hold a claim for him on shares—now known as the Holmes farm. It was promised and understood that as soon as Mr. Twogood's house was finished, he would look out a claim for me. Mr. Twogood and I started for the woods to get everything ready. The trees had been felled, hewn to a thickness of six inches, roofing gotten out, and logs hauled to the site. When this was done, the cabin raised and made comfortable, Mr. Twogood moved in.

In the meantime Mr. Haight pointed out to me the quarter sections where Col. Marsh, Mr. Perry, Mr. John Lake, and many others have since built, but there was no timber, although he thought I might be able to purchase a piece of timber—which I did in the fall. Mr. Haight gave me permission to go into his timber and take all I wanted for my house. As I had helped Mr. Twogood with his house, he helped me with mine. We felled enough timber to build a house 18x24 feet, and got out shakes enough to cover it, and when everything was in readiness, we reported to Mr. Haight. He sent his teams over in the morning. We had the material hauled to my land, and the house raised and completed before sunset. Mr. Haight took full charge of the work, and is the best man on a log house I ever saw.

My family remained in Mr. Haight's house till I had mine finished, as far as we could at that time. In leaving Chicago the roads were very rough, so I bought two wide pine boards to prevent my things from being jolted out and lost. This was fortunate, for they were enough to make my door and sash. The house was a story and a half; no floor below or above—not a board could I get. I applied to my old friend, Mr. Haight, to allow me to go into his woods and take down some basswood trees for the bark; this was readily granted. Fortunately for me, it was just at the right time, and I could get it off the full length across my house; so I spread it out without much difficulty, and pinned it down. I doubt if any lady in town to-day rejoiced more over a new carpet than my wife did over hers. I got in a little patch for a garden.

The first frame building was put up by Mr. Twogood and myself, for a store for Goodhue & Bundy, whose goods were then stored in Mr. Haight's log stable. It was raised as post and beam, all prepared with the axe in the woods; siding gotten out with a cooper's frow in four feet lengths, shaved down to a thickness; shingles were of oak, made on the spot. The building was put up on the south-west corner of State and Madison streets, opposite the present Y. M. C. A. building, and was afterwards bought and occupied by Potter & Preston. The building now stands close to the railroad, on the south side of State street.

We put up the second building, as a residence for Mr. Haight, on the north-east corner of the same streets; the house and garden at one time occupied that whole block. It now stands at the corner south of Mr. J. Early.

Then came the Rockford House, opened and kept by Mr. Thurston.

At this time settlers began to come in very fast, and the few first settlers felt uneasy about their claims, and some wanted to "unload," provided they could get their price, which was more than the land would bring for years after. A great many claim-holders hung around "seeking whom they might devour." If a wagon hove in sight, they would hold a council and decide what to do. A great deal of sympathy was often exhibited for the poor, tired-out family. The next thing was to know how the exchequer stood. If that was found to be low, the teams, wagons, etc., were closely scrutinized. After a little friendly talk the traveler would enquire if they knew where he could make a claim. "No, sir, it is all taken." "Why, I saw no house for miles on the road, in my journey over the prairies." "All taken, all taken! What kind of a claim do you wish?" On having this question answered, they would inform him that he could be accommodated, possibly, if he would stop for a few days and rest, but they "would be too busy until to-morrow." To-morrow, if they were not too lazy, some one would start off with an axe, prepared to mark off a claim for his new found friend, extolling the country and telling how fast land is going up, till he has him well soaped and greased, all ready to swallow, wagons and all.

I think there was a state law at this time, securing to an actual settler his claim of 160 acres, and a strong hope that congress would pass a pre-emption law granting 160 acres to all American citizens; but it did not.

With the large claim holders there seems to have been, about this time, a cloud about the size of a man's hand showing above the horizon. They did not know how soon their boundaries might be lessened. "In union," it is said, "there is strength," and not knowing how soon the gathering storm might burst, a meeting was called, and the big holders were prompt to respond. "United we stand, divided we fall," was perhaps their motto. A compact was entered into, by-laws framed and signed by the squatters, including some who had purchased their claims, as they felt a little sore at being so nicely skinned, and perhaps their purchases amounted to a section or more. One of those gentlemen claim-dealers, at one of the meetings, mounting an oak stump, delivered himself thusly: "Gentlemen, when we see a family come among us, we will take a look at them, and if their looks suit us, well; if not, tell him he can't stay; and he can't." At another time the same gentleman delivered himself thusly: "I have made $1,500 without dirtying my fingers." So it was not a bad business with some. But in looking around, where are many of those land pirates now? Echo answers "where?" Many of them did not pay their debts, and many of them do not own a foot of land to-day; and some are where we do not wish to disturb them.

CHAPTER III.

Mr. Lake's Narrative Continued—A Mile of Fence Moved in One Night—The Field of Battle—Mr. Brown Defends his Castle—Stampede of the Crowd at the Appearance of a Rifle Barrel—A Truce—Land Speculators—The Last Piece of Bread—Kent Divides his Flour—Flour $22 per Barrel—Butter Required to Cook Pork—Greyhound Breed of Hogs—A Rifle Ball Required to Stop Them—First Ball—Table Service—The Menu of Bacheler's Hall—Prairie Itch—Hog's Ears, Snouts and Tails—Tailoring—First Tailor—First Blacksmith—First Shoemaker—Carpenters and Joiners—First Brick—First Lime—Midway—Dr. Goodhue Author of the Name "Rockford"—Low Prices—Couldn't Cast a Shadow—First Cannon—Hickory Pole—'Rah for Jackson.

Now do not think those large claim-holders had no difficulties among themselves. Far from it. Occasionally they would be very industrious; move perhaps a mile or more of fence, in the middle of the night, off their own claims on to their neighbor's, and have it all nicely laid up by morning. Then, a few nights after, those rails would be, by some hocuspocus, all hurled in heaps and set on fire. What a sight, a line of fire extending for nearly a mile, by morning ashes instead of rails. Then again, by way of change, while a man slept his whole farm would be sown, not to tares, but to buckwheat; or, some poor traveler, not having money to buy a claim, would venture, in some out-of-the-way place, to put up a cabin. Then the wrath of the mighty conclave would be stirred, a meeting called, a day appointed, and his house pulled down and burned.

Just here a case of that kind will work in to show the height of our civilization. In the winter of 1837, a person arrived in our midst named Brown, (not John Brown, of Harper's Ferry,) having a family of seven children, one an infant. They were but poorly stocked with clothes, and worse with provisions; but then they owned a choice span of mares and a tolerably good wagon. Having little or no money, they wished to make a claim and settle down. The usual sound greeted their ears: "No claim, sir; all taken. But I can sell you one." They concluded to look around and see if they could not find a spot far enough away from any one to allow them to settle down and live in peace. This was soon done, to his satisfaction, and there he built himself a log cabin, and moved out of his wagon into his new home, when he was informed that his castle was to be pulled down, as the claim belonged to Mr. Spaulding, being in St. Louis. Mr. Brown, they soon found out, was not composed of milk and water, so to get him out of the way a plan was laid to entice him to Rockford under the pretext that a gentleman wished to buy his team. Perhaps the birds overheard the plans, for when the noble envoy arrived and delivered his message, Mr. Brown coolly informed him that he should be pleased to sell his team, but that he was not going to Rockford just then. This plan foiled, they were forced to try another—the last resort, and one that seldom failed. A band of the faithful was called together—whiskey was plenty and that made help plenty. Brown, by some unaccountable means, kept posted, and prepared for an assault. Soon after noon on the day appointed, the faithful began to collect, and as the cordial passed down in full bumpers their courage rose. The teams were all ready, and the valiant crew began to fill the seats. Amid the blare of horns, the beating of kettles, and shouts, the order was given to march to the field of battle. Arriving at Brown's, they formed in line of march and approached somewhat nearer the castle. A truce was called and Brown asked to surrender. Brown, not seeing it in that light, opened a port and thrust out a musket. The ranks broke and a stampede for the woods occurred. Mrs. Brown began to fear for their safety, knowing the preparations that had been made and the determination of her husband to defend them to the last, that many of them would probably be killed and they all murdered, persuaded her husband to capitulate, if he could make favorable terms. Brown, still within the house, consented to hear their terms. "If you will leave this claim we agree to get you a better one, build you a house, and furnish you with provisions." The terms were accepted and the barricade taken away, when a rush was made for the house, and all the effects taken out, the house torn down, the logs rolled together and set on fire. The cordial getting low about this time, many began looking toward Rockford. Brown's family and effects were loaded on the wagon and taken for a short distance into the woods, where they were left to shift for themselves, the rabble returning to headquarters.

At this time it was cold, but clear, through the night snow fell to the depth of six or eight inches. Some kind friends took compassion on them and gave them shelter for the night. On the return of Mr. Spaulding, he denied ever having any pretensions to ownership of the claim, and any one who knew him would readily believe it, for he was too good a judge to accept any such claim, as any one could see by the number and quality of those he held.

It was not an uncommon thing, in those days, for a man to use his employes to hold claims. It was said by some that one of Mr. Spaulding's claims was marked by a furrow, drawn somewhere above the ferry and extending to Pecatonica, including all between the furrow and the river. The furrow I have seen, but the north end was too far for my curiosity; there was too much walking to be done.

Mr. Haight's house being pretty well under way, Twogood and I entered into a contract with a gentleman, well known as Charley Reed, to erect a tavern at the then county seat, Winnebago. According to the condition of the contract, the material to finish off with was to be sent from Chicago. Nothing was seen of Reed until late in the spring. The tavern was already raised. In the raising I was accidentally injured by one of the men letting fall a big maul on my head, in the act of catching a pin, which caused a fracture of the skull and laid me up for a long time, under the care of Dr. Whitney, of Belvidere. At one time it was doubted if I would recover.

Some may think there was no organized religion at this early settlement. Had they attended the old settlers first meetings on the fair grounds, they would have been convinced to the contrary, as the public were then told that they, the first settlers, brought their religion with them. One Saturday evening one of the leaders of the church called at my house and inquired of my wife as to the health of her husband. Being informed that the doctor had just left, and he thought he was some little better, the good man left. The next day, Sabbath, there was quite a meeting held, with a strong religious feeling manifested, with supplication, undoubtedly, for strength, for there was work to be done, and that quickly, for it may be the sick man might recover, and there were some thousands of rails to move from one of the brother's claims that joined the sick man's, whilst he was safe in bed. After much praying and little fasting, as the work had to be done that night, the brethren were dismissed, to meet again later in the evening. True to agreement, all were on hand except one, as report had it; he, the poorest of the brethren in worldly goods, refused to attend, as he thought their deeds were evil, consequently he was stricken from the rolls of the brethren, and told to ask no favors. The sick man's wife, having had but little rest during the illness of her husband, and he feeling a little better, slept soundly. The first thing on going to the door about sunrise Monday morning, she saw a fence running near the house leaving about fifteen acres; there was up to this line eighty to ninety acres on his claim, and the greater part laid to seed, but this was disregarded, and his fence was thrown on one side when in the brethren's way. The sick man recovered, and went on to fence, paying but little attention to the night work. He had all his fence put up and his crop planted on about forty acres. Now came the tug of war. After the crop got up, whilst the owner was at work, the fence would often be pulled down and the cattle turned in; if the water was high enough, one of the brethren would throw the rails into the creek and another would stand below and haul them out, as they floated down stream. Working hard by day and watching cattle nights, and sometimes having to rebuild forty or fifty rods of fence, did not add to his strength or mellow his temper. He began to doubt if it would hold him in check much longer. At this juncture, an old man named Clark, known afterward as the "Old Johnny" Clark, dropped into the building, inquiring for work. After thinking a moment I determined, if it was possible, I would save a part of my crop. After telling him I could give him work, and explaining to him what I wished him to do, and its difficulties; that he was to watch my crops nights, keep up the fence if possible, to do what he chose through the day, sleep as long as he wished—I to furnish a horse, board and washing for him, and $16 per month. It was just the thing that suited him he said. His being up nights was no objection, as he he was an old man, and was weak, and rather liked the fun. There were always refreshments set on the table at our retiring at night. "Old Johnny" would come in, help himself quietly—sometimes we did not hear him— and then quickly mount his horse and go his rounds. Sometimes he said he would not be over fifteen minutes, and perhaps thirty to fifty rods of fence would be pulled down, and thirty to forty head of cattle turned in. He would get awful mad, and beg me to let him have my gun—he would make a fence, he said. "No sir; I pay you your wages. You can have no gun of mine; you would get into trouble. I hire you to keep me out of trouble." At last, lightning had struck a pair of oxen, and in burying them, marks of galena were found, and I supposed a mineral abounded on the claim. Cattle did not trouble me much after that. This claim ended in a law suit, but the brethren could not all get on the jury, and so failed to agree. So the law suit ended.

I have more than fifteen acres of land now, and have so far, paid my debts. That is more than some of those midnight brethren have, or have done. This is but a very light sketch of the proceedings of those days. But I will try to abide by a certain injunction a lady gave the speaker appointed at the first Old Settlers' meeting, "Don't tell all you know." But as the name familiar in those days, of "Charley Reed" is but little known to the present inhabitants, we will just look at him a little. Friend Charley was quite a pleasant old gentleman, lived perhaps somewhere about Joliet, rode a good horse, was well but plainly dressed, carried a small hatchet—perhaps it was not the one Washington cut down his father's cherry tree with, but a hatchet. Thus equipped, his periodical wanderings were over the prairies and through the woods, from Fox river to Apple river, and often beyond, selecting and marking claims, of which he was a good judge. The mark of his hatchet he could point out to you on many choice pieces of timber; on the prairie it was more trouble, as perhaps it would require a few poles, or rails, if a very choice and large one; sometimes it was taken possession of by merely riding across. These long journeys were undertaken as often as business required his presence, or to sell off a piece occasionally. As Charley was a good judge, in his absence some one would settle down on his claims, build a house, plow, etc. This would start Charley's ire. He would get cross and threaten vengeance; he would bid in the land at the land sale if you did not hand over a thousand or so. This was vexation of spirit, and he must keep some one to attend to his business about Rockford, as it could not be expected of a man to be at Fox river, Apple river, and all intermediate points, at one and the same time. His son was sent out and established at Rockford and vicinity —a very nice and agreeable young man. As he and the writer often worked together, I got well posted on his father's business. But many, not having the fear of Charley before their eyes, still transgressed by making homes of some of his waste land property; and at the land sale Charley's cash run low, as was the case with many others at the land sale. But few of the actual settlers were prepared with money. Of stock and grain many had plenty, but neither could be sold for money. If any one owed you he would not pay, as money was worth thirty per cent. Some had their claims bid in on shares, and much more was bid in by monied men, on condition to double in three years—33⅓ per cent.—the one furnishing the money as his own, and giving a bond to the claimant to redeem at the expiration of three years, if the money was paid prior to or on that day. The money loaner fully supposed his title was good, as it was entered in his own name and paid for in full with his money; but it was decided otherwise by the supreme court; it was treated as a mortgage. There was much lawing on the question, and much money spent.

Many of the foregoing remarks would not have been made, had not some writers endeavored to make it appear that all was harmony, good feeling, and peace and quietness in those days; but how often could the heavens be seen lighted by the destruction of some poor man's cabin, where he had toiled and fought both hunger and cold, to make a home for the little ones, and on this very claim, prior to his, there was no mark to show that a man had ever set foot. Such is life!

At times, provisions ran very low. I remember, returning from my work on Mr. Haight's house one evening, I had had no dinner; my wife set a small piece of bread on the table, and a little butter, and a cup of tea, with the remark, "I don't know what we shall do, for that piece of bread, and what I am to bake," which she had made up ready for the oven, "is all we have." The loaf, or cake mentioned was about the size of a pint bowl. I knew we were running short, but did not know we were so reduced. I left the table immediately, without tasting a mouthful, returned to Rockford and called on Mr. Haight and stated our situation. I was sorrowfully told by him that he could not possibly help us in the least, as he was situated much like ourselves. I started for the river and hailed a boat. When I was ferried across, I made for Mr. Kent's and told him as I told Mr. Haight. The same reply, "I can't help you with a pound. Come and see." He lifted the cover from a flour barrel and stated how many he had to feed, and knowing well, if either had any to spare I could get it in a moment, I turned away sorrowfully to return. Mr. Kent plainly saw my suffering of mind, and called me back. "Mr. Lake, you shall not go so; I will let you have a little." I held open a little bag, he took a very little plate and dipped out of the barrel a few times, looking closely after every dip, knowing he was doing what he ought not to do in justice to himself. Weighed it; there were twelve pounds. I asked the price; he hesitated, at last he said one dollar and fifty-five cents. I never paid money, I think, so cheerfully as I did this. A few days after I saw a large Hoosier wagon coming down the hill toward the river. Hope and fear were about equally balanced in my mind. They may have flour on board. Before they fairly stopped, I hurriedly asked, "What have you on board?" "Flour." "What do you ask?" "Twenty-two dollars per barrel." "Roll me out three barrels." Here I made a mistake, for it soon fell to $16, but I had flour. Having hands to work for me it was necessary to have meat also. I started for Savana with a team; there I bought some pork and other necessaries of a Mr. Brown. Hoosier pork, smoked black, about the thickness of a man's hand, and resembled a piece of old oak slab that had lain around for years; but we found butter would cook it. At another time, standing below the old Rockford house site, in company with a man named Strand, who had arrived with a drove of hogs of the greyhound breed, to be fattened on prairie grass, or what they could pick up, our supply of meat about out, and one of them cropping grass in the road, and having a good rifle in his hand, and being a good shot, I asked him what he would take for that hog. "A shilling a pound," he answered, "just as he is." "Stop him," I said—no sooner said than done. He was a racer, and nothing short of lead could overtake him, as he was making two-forty for the brush, but he dropped with a squeal. I hooked him on Mr. Haight's steel-yard; handed over Mr. Strand one shilling a pound, and got him loaded for home. When dressed he would have made a good lantern, much better than for cooking. It was a sad excuse for pork, but with difficulty we picked his bones.

The first ball in Rockford was held in Mr. Haight's new building, at his request. Had to remove the partitions and remove our benches and materials, doors, casings, etc., to make room. Quite a crowd attended from a great many miles around. It was a benefit for Mr. Thurston, as he had leased the Rockford House when built. Mr.

Thurston's family not being here, Mrs. Haight, Mrs. Twogood and Mrs. Lake, and perhaps some others now forgotten, did the cooking. The materials were furnished by Mr. Thurston. Table service being short, small pieces of board answered the purpose of trays, plates, etc. Had a good time, and dancing kept up until the small hours. The arrangement could not have fallen into better hands than Mr. Thurston, as this was not his first attempt at providing for a jovial party, but not always carried out in such splendor and display, perhaps, as on this occasion. Could it be acted out again now, in the same style, it would require a larger hall than Brown's the second night, so perhaps it had not best be attempted till the walls of the new court house are up."

While my father and I were keeping bachelor's hall in the Vance cabin, as will readily occur to the reader, our bill of fare was limited. We had no vegetables, and aside from an occasional duck which I potted in the river, the menu comprised, for breakfast, fried bacon and bread; for dinner, bread and bacon fried; and for supper, something that might be quickly got together, which usually was some preparation of bacon. We had fish lines set on the bank of the river and occasionally got a cat fish. There was a species of wild onion growing on the banks of the river, about half the size of a lead pencil, which I gathered and ate with avidity.

One institution peculiar to 1837-8, has never been recorded to my knowledge—"The Prairie Itch"!!! Soon after our arrival I innocently asked my father "what was the matter with Mr. Haight's hands." "He's got the itch, you little fool, and don't you open your head about it." Everybody had it; I had it, my father got it before I did, being required to shake hands, my brother had it, my sister caught it, we all were afflicted except my mother, who escaped. It was epidemic. "Old Frost," who was a Jack at all trades, and professed to some knowledge of medicine, made an ointment that was, I think, some decoction of tobacco, and did temporarily ease up the scratching, but it was universal until the arrival of Dr. Goodhue, in the fall of 1838, when he made anguintum by the pailful, and exterminated the malady.

Mr. S. D. Gregory has supplied me with a copy of a letter written in December, 1836, by his father, Samuel Gregory, to his brother in Lockport, N. Y., in which he mentions not only the prairie itch, but also various interesting items of pioneer life, which is here appended:

ROCKFORD, Ill., Dec. 20, 1836.

DEAR BROTHER EPHRAIM:—With pleasure I now spend a little time in writing to let you know that we are yet alive, and amidst surrounding mercies enjoying good health, excepting colds and the prairie itch, which is some like having the seven year itch all at once; we are getting better of that. We are well suited with the country, for a more excellent soil of land I have never seen; I have fears that winter wheat will not do well, the winters are so open that it kills out.

I have sown five bushels for a trial. Summer crops grow abundantly. Have been hauling rails to fence 160 acres, on which I have 30 acres broke. Wages are from $20 to $25 per month for the year. Provisions are very high—flour $15 to $20 per barrel. Hoosier hog meat $8 per hundred. Beef five and six cents per pound, of which we use much. The weather is cold; about eight inches of snow.

If you can find two or three men that will come to Illinois and work for us, we will pay them $17 per month by the year; if good hands will pay their expenses if they come within six months. Tell brother Harry if he can collect some money on the notes I left him, I would like to buy some cows, as butter and cheese bring a big price. Cheese 1s. 6d., butter 25 to 35 cents per pound. Tell Harry to send large bills, cutting them in two and directing one package to Eliphelet and the other to me. Hoping to see you soon,

Your brother,
SAMUEL GREGORY.

At Mr. Benj. T. Lee's place on the Cherry Valley road, where it meets the timber, he had three men employed. When I arrived the only meat they possessed was a barrel of hogs' ears, snouts and tails. I was there several days while this meat was being consumed, and can testify to the good quality and generous proportions of the tails, but the ears, like the tails as to size, were stringy, and the snouts most unwieldy objects to carve, being of the consistency of India rubber when not thoroughly cooked, which was sometimes the case. Fortunately we did not depend on store teeth.

We had a cow, and at a time when the hired man was unable to work in the field, he and I determined to have some butter. Securing a small amount of cream, we stirred it with a spoon in a pitcher, at intervals, for a day and a half before we succeeded. This was the first butter I saw in Rockford. From necessity we had traveled with a light amount of baggage, and soon after my arrival the seams ripped of the only pair of trousers I had. Mrs. Haight supplied me with thread and needles, and retiring to a sequestered place I doffed the garment and made my first essay at tailoring. I sewed them over and over, making a round, whiplash-like seam, which although somewhat inconvenient when I sat down, was substantial.

The first tailor in Rockford was William H. Tinker, from Massachusetts, now of St. Paul, Minn., who was here in 1836, but not finding the outlook promising, had abandoned the field. Mr. Parson King Johnson, from Brandon, Vermont, now of Mankato, Minn., came here in June, 1837, and writes me he found Tinker's cutting board in the back room of Bundy & Goodhue's store. Mr. Tinker returning soon after, they joined forces, and the firm of Tinker & Johnson (Little Johnson,) blossomed as the first business house in that line in the town. They occupied the upper room in a building on the site of 111 South Madison street.

The first blacksmith, I presume was one of Kent's men, and I have previously located the log hut used for a shop. William Penfield was the only blacksmith when I came; his shop I have elsewhere located. William P. Dennis, of our party, was the first house painter, and his work in 1837 upon Haight's dwelling, opposite the Rockford House, was not equalled for some years after.

The first shoemaker was Ezra Barnum, from Danbury, Conn., (the father of Anson Barnum, afterwards a prominent man in the county,) who arrived early in the summer of 1837. There was no new leather to be had, at least I concluded so, for I remember some repairs he made upon my shoes, using old boot legs.

Of house carpenters and joiners, it may be difficult to decide who were the first, but I think Thos. Lake and Sidney Twogood may claim to have been the first skilled workmen. They built Haight's barn and his dwelling house, the house having a winding stair and banister rail. This house is now standing on the northeast corner of Second and Walnut streets.

Cyrus C. Jenks made the first brick in the fall of 1837 at his claim in Guilford, about three and a half miles northeast of the town. This question of the first brick came up some fifteen years ago, and as illustrating the vivid recollections of a boy, none of the early settlers could identify the maker until I stated it was the first brick kiln I ever saw. Most of these brick were used for chimnies. The first brick house in the county was a small, one story square structure on the southeast corner of block 18, on First street, opposite the public square, built in 1838 by a Mr. John H. Morse, who soon afterwards went to St. Louis to reside.

Mrs. Harriet Hard, of Guilford, supplies me with this item in regard to the first lime burned in the county. "Giles says the lime used to plaster Bundy & Goodhue's store was burned on a pile of logs heaped up near the northwest corner of the Cedar Bluff cemetery, by one of the Boswells. He piled limestone on the log-heap and set the timber on fire, obtaining sufficient lime to use about the store. This was in the fall of 1836. In the spring of 1837, Deacon Holt, of Westfield, burned a kiln of lime which turned out about 200 bushels, disposing of the entire lot to Daniel S. Haight and Giles, who was in Haight's employ, hauled it to Rockford, where it was used upon his dwelling and the Rockford House." A word here about the name "Midway" as designating the town in the 30's, and so persistently advertised by the city editor of one of the local papers. I never heard the name until recent years, and have it from James B. Martyn personally, that Kent, in writing to him at Huntsville, Ala., stated the locality as about midway between Chicago and Galena, and suggested that Midway might be a good name for the embryo town which he hoped would some day prove a reality. It will be seen by

Mr. Thomas Lake's reminiscences, the town bore its present designation when he arrived. Doctor Josiah C. Goodhue, who came here from Chicago in the fall of 1838, and who was interested in the town plat on the East Side, was author of the name Rockford, and it was so called when I arrived.

The immigration to this locality in the years 1837-8 was simply immense, a regular "boom." The roads were thronged with immigrants, many of them driving cattle, horses and hogs, and as each had a little money, trade was excellent. How sadly this fell off may be appreciated, when I state that in the fall of '40, a bushel of wheat could not be exchanged for a pound of loaf sugar. Wheat was accepted by the local dealers for dry goods, but cash was required for groceries. An excellent cow could be purchased at from eight to ten dollars, a good horse for forty, or practically at such price as the cash buyer chose to dictate.

In the early forties the people of this county were so poor they "couldn't cast a shadow," to use a most appropriate expression of "Judge" E. S. Blackstone. I venture to say that in 1841-2 there were not twenty farmers in the county who possessed a suit of clothes suitable to wear to church or to court, which they had purchased with the avails of labor on their farms. Alas for those among the settlers who had passed their prime physically. Too old to withstand the hardships of pioneer life, they sickened, and in some instances they straggled back to the old homes at the east to die. Among the latter were my own parents, leaving me in 1842 to fight the battle of life alone. Was I contented and happy? Yes I was; a boy with a shotgun

The first cannon used in the town we made ourselves. When I say "we," I mean that I personally assisted in its construction. Wm. Penfield's anvil had a hole in the bottom and we drilled a touch hole to the implement, making a safe piece of ordinance to be used for the first Fourth of July celebration in 1837, which was indeed a grand affair, not exceeded since then in noise and patriotic demonstrations. As preliminary to the event a young cow was purchased early in the summer for a meat supply, and shortly before the day, Giles C. Hard (still among us,) went to the woods for a pole. Giles' predilections were for an ash pole, the emblem of the whigs, but being a young man in those days, not so wise as he has since become, he was overpersuaded by older and possibly more sagacious democrats, who insisted that the event to come off had no political significance. He returned with a hickory pole, which being placed in position, the crowd by previous arrangement gathered about, and to the infinite chagrin of Giles, as the stars and stripes went aloft, burst out, in which I heartily joined, with, "'Rah for Jackson, 'Rah!"

CHAPTER IV.

First Fourth of July Celebration—Tickets One Dollar—Zip Coon—"Jake, for ——'s Jake, don't Play so Fast"—First Rope for Ferry—First Dancing School—"Go Ahead, First Four"—"Couldn't git to Dance with Her"—First Drug Store—Seventy Grains of Calomel—First School—Early Teachers—Rockford House Opened—Actors, Authors, Poets—Sobriquets—Claim Jumping—"China" Parker—Electrical Disturbances—Rings on the Prairie—"The Buffalo Made 'Em—First Butcher—A Banker Fisherman—First Circuit Court—First Court House—Distinguished Lawyers—Long John's Maiden Speech—"To Congress, by ——"—Hon. R. R. Hitt's Letter—Postmaster General's Letter—First Postmaster—First P. O. Building—No Key to open the Mail-bag—P. O. Box 100—Joe Jefferson.

My father, with such assistance as I could render, cooked the dinner in Mrs. Haight's large iron kettle. It was of bread and beef, *a la mode* and otherwise. The main part of the Rockford House had the roof on and was sided up to the first story windows; some loose boards were laid for a floor, tables erected, and the cold meat served on clean shingles, for want of crockery. There was an occasional butcher knife for carving purposes, but each guest was expected to, and did provide his own cutlery, Tickets were one dollar each, and as every patriot of the male persuasion became a purchaser, the result proved a financial success. The morning of Independence Day, 1837, was ushered in by the boom of the cannon fired as rapidly as the gunners could load it. The speaking was done in Haight's barn, the bay being floored over for the speakers, and the threshing floor occupied by the ladies and distinguished (?) guests. Charles I. Horseman read the Declaration of Independence and John C. Kemble was orator of the day. The whole wound up with a grand ball, the first in Winnebago county, held in Haight's house. Some shirting was tacked to the studding about one room for a ladies' dressing room, and with an orchestra of three fiddles, led by Old Jake Miller, whose only dancing tune was Zip Coon, "the mirth and fun grew fast and furious," every little while some perspiring fellow rushing to the orchestra and exclaiming, "Jake, for ——'s sake, don't play so fast."

The first rope provided for the ferry, was about the first of June, 1837, as I recollect hauling lumber from Kent's mill at that time, and also that the rope was new. It was fastened to a burr oak tree on the east bank about one hundred feet above State street, and to a frame work on the west shore. In warm weather we usually crossed at the ford, the water coming just above the forward axle of a wagon, not varying more than six inches in depth for the entire distance.

The young people among the early settlers were most devoted followers of Terpsichore, the result being that "Old Hayes," (Andrew Lovejoy,) who was an accomplished musician, secured a large number of scholars for a dancing school, the first in the county, in the winter of 1837-8. The Hoosiers not having been trained in the square figures which the Yankees introduced, were the cause of some ludicrous incidents. One of them, who with his girl always came on horseback, was on the side set of a cotillion for the first dance. As the music started he sang out, "Hayes, Hayes, hold on; wait till I git my pumps on!" He sat down on the bench behind him, took his pumps and stockings from his coat tail pocket, pulled off his boots and stockings, kicked them under the bench, and as he drew on the second stocking called out, "Go ahead, first four, I'll be ready!" On another occasion, a young fellow who brought a pretty girl whom the town boys were disposed to monopolize, had been unable to secure her for a partner during the evening, and the last set was on the floor. The case being desperate, he accosted her partner, exclaiming, "Tut, you've got my gall. I fotched her clean all the way from Kishwauk, and couldn't git to dance with her yit!"

The first drug store was opened early in the summer of 1838, in a small frame building on the north side of State street, about eighty feet from the river shore, by a Doctor (?) Marshall, a Scotchman, who I have recently learned was a genuine quack, and who probably made it go hard with some of his patients. He was called to prescribe for Doctor Haskell, who refused to take his medicine, which proved to be 70 grains of calomel.

The first school in this county was held on the site of 110 South Second street, by Miss Eunice Brown, in a log cabin, at which my brother attended. Another scholar I recall was Miss Mary Barnum, (she became the first wife of the late Jonathan T. Miller,) a daughter of Ezra Barnum. A most complete list of the schools of Rockford was compiled (and is here inserted) with much labor and care by my deceased wife for publication in the Rockford City Directory for 1869, which may be accepted as substantially correct. It was a subject in which she felt warmly interested, and but for her labor at that time many of the facts related would have been lost.

From the Rockford City Directory for 1869:

"A lady of this city who has lived in or near it from its earliest times, deeming that it should be known that education has always received encouragement here; that we have always had good schools, and that the public interest in education did not commence with the present school system, has, at a very considerable expenditure of time and labor, obtained the following school statistics of the city, showing as far as she could get, the proper information, the names of all teachers who have taught in Rockford, and the time and place of teaching, which we have endeavored to put in proper shape for publication.

"Miss Eunice Brown, now Mrs. J. G. Lyon, of the town of Rockton, in this county, was the first teacher who taught a school here. She first taught in the summer of 1837, in a log cabin that stood on the premises now owned by Mr. John Early, near the southeast corner of State and Second streets, east side, and afterwards on the west side in several different places.

"Miss Frances Bradford also taught school in 1837, on the west side, in a log cabin belonging to the late Wm. E. Dunbar, that stood a short distance south of the present residence of S. C. Withrow, in South Rockford. These two ladies were the pioneer teachers of the city.

"Israel Morrill and Miss Sarah E. Danforth taught in 1838 on the west side, Miss Wood in 1839 on the west side, Jas. M. Wight in the winter of 1838-9, in a building on the corner of Main and Market streets, east side, the present site of the American House, Miss Hyde in 1839, in the same place, Andrus Corbin in 1839, in a house owned by himself, on the west side, Mr. Jackson in the winter of 1839-40, in the house corner of Main and Market streets, east side, Miss Hepsabeth Hutchinson and Miss Maria Baker in 1840, on the east side, Mrs. Mary Jackson in 1838-9, on the west side, Miss Wealthy Bradford in 1841-42, on the west side, Lewis S. Sweezy in 1841-2, in the brick school house that stood on the southeast corner of the public square, east side, Miss Harriet Barnum in 1841, in a private house, east side, Miss Minerva C. Fletcher in 1842, in a log house that stood opposite the First Congregational church, east side. Elijah Holt in 1841-2, in brick school house, east side. John Paul in 1841, in the first house south of the railroad, Main street, west side. Lewis B. Gregory in 1843-4, in brick school house, east side. Miss Fronia Foot and George Waterman in 1843-4, Miss Julia Barnum in 1844, in private house, east side. Miss Adaline Warren, private house, east side. Miss Augusta Kemfield in 1845, east side. C. A. Huntington, from 1845 to 1849, in the old court house that stood on the northwest corner of Market and First streets, east side, and from 1849 to 1851 in the Baptist church, west side. Miss Elizabeth Weldon, assistant to Mr. Huntington. H. H. Waldo in 1848, in Baptist church, west side. D. W. Ticknor from 1846 to 1849, in the brick school house, southeast corner of public square east side assisted by Miss Elizabeth Weldon,

Anson Barnum, John W. Andrews and D. Dubois. H. H. Waldo in 1849-50. Miss Hannah Morrill in 1848, east side. Robert A. Sanford in 1848, west side.

"The Rockford Female Seminary was first organized in May, 1849, under the present efficient principal, Miss Anna P. Sill, with the Misses Hannah and Eliza Richards as assistants, and Miss Melinda Richards in 1850. They occupied the old court house, east side.

"Mr. Bowles in 1850, in the brick school house, east side. Mrs. Squiers in 1850, in what is now No. 111 Main street, east side, afterwards on west side. Mrs. King H. Milliken in 1850, east side. Miss Mary Dow, Miss Delia Hyde and George E. Kimball in 1850 to 1853, in basement of the Baptist church, west side. Miss Sarah A. Stewart and Miss Mary Joslin in 1850, in a building where the Holland House now stands. Seely Perry in the basement of the Second street Methodist church, east side; quite a number of his pupils pursued the usual studies of the Freshman class, and entered Beloit College one year in advance. B. Rush Catlin in 1852, in the basement of the Second street Methodist church, east side. Misses Charlotte and Harriet Leonard in 1851-2. Miss Stowell and T. J. L. Remington in 1851, in the brick school house, west side. Rev. C. Reighty in 1852, on the east side. Miss Fanny Avery in 1852 on the east side. Mr. Stevens in 1853 in the brick school house, east side. In the Classic Institute, located in the basement of the Baptist church, on the west side, from 1853 to 1856, of which Henry P. Kimball was principal, one class pursued the usual studies of the freshman year in college and entered one year in advance. A score of students left this institution and entered eastern colleges. Two years study was considered sufficient to advance scholars through a full preparatory course of mathematics and the usual books in Latin and Greek, giving them a thorough and sufficient preparation. Miss Lizzie Frow, in 1853, on the east side. Mrs. Carpenter, in 1853 on the west side. Rev. L. Porter in 1852, Mr. Stowell in 1853, Rev. Addison Brown and Miss Frances A. Brown in 1854, in a school house built by John A. Holland, south of the residence of T. D. Robertson, west side. Miss Julia Galloway in 1854, in lobby of the First Congregational church, east side. Darwin Dubois, in 1854, in Second street Methodist church, east side. Mrs. Julia and Miss Chapman in 1854, on west side, Miss Belle Burpee and Miss Ethalinda Thompson, in 1855 on the east side. Halsey G. Clark in 1855, in the old court house, east side, with Miss Lizzie Giffin as assistant. Miss Emma Brown in 1857 on the east side, ———Freeman in the basement of the Baptist church west side, Wesley Sovereign in Second street Methodist church, east side. Mrs Jones on west side. Miss Elizabeth Fisher, west side, Miss Gunsolus, east side, Mr. Johnson and Mr. Gifford, west side."

Late in the fall of 1837, the wing of the Rockford House was finished and Henry Thurston opened the hotel, it being the first framed structure erected for hotel use in Winnebago county. There was no way of getting to the third story of the house which was divided into two rooms, except by a ladder made from slats nailed to two pieces of the studding in the first story of the main building. It was a part of my duty that winter to make the beds and escort the guests of the house up that ladder when they retired. I was specially charged not to drop the melted tallow from the dip which I carried up the ladder onto the party who followed me.

We were wholly dependent upon ourselves for amusement in those days, even the circus was yet in the distant future. The long evenings in winter were tedious. We had but little to read and although we played whist, seven-up and some of the boys played a strong hand at a game similar to what is now draw poker, still at times, it was exceedingly dull and various expedients were resorted to by which to while away the hours. Possibly we might never have known of the dormant talent in our midst, had not necessity brought it out. We had actors, authors, artists, orators and poets of ability, and we graduated—at least some of us did—into a community of story tellers.

Every fellow, old and young, had his sobriquet, to which he responded as promptly as when addressed by his proper name. My own was "Uncle John," to my infinite annoyance. Among those I recall there was Old Hayes, (after the noted thief catcher in New York,) Big Johnson, Little Johnson, China, Blowser, Flint, Gunlock, Tut, S C, Queen, with others who may not be named to ears polite, and a father with four sons, known as Old Frost, Young Frost, Big Frost, Little Frost and Red Frost. Some twenty-five years ago I saw an emigrant's team standing in front of William Worthington's store on State street, and knew from the style of the outfit that the proprietor was a pioneer. Going into the store I recognized and accosted him. "Sir," said I, "you resemble a man whom I knew many years ago, and I think you are Red Frost." "That's the man, by ——, who in Sheol are you?"

Claim jumping was a profession among a few of the early inhabitants. Others there were who "jumped" a claim for honest settlement. Among the last named class was the late William Peters. With old Rob and Tanner I conveyed him and a load of lumber, in the fall of 1837, to the claim he "jumped" in Guilford, and which his executors sold recently at some eighty or more dollars per acre.

"China" Parker was one of the professionals, and a fighter from away back on the Picktonick(that's one way it was spelled)bottoms. At one time he was bound over to court, and as he could not furnish bail, there being no jail here, Haight, the sheriff, with "Old Hayes" and "Queen" as guards, took him to Galena and placed him in the lockup there. "China" made his appearance in town at 10 o'clock the evening previous to the arrival home of his guards. For explanation, he told us he was sitting at an upper window in the evening, and dropping asleep fell out, landing upon a cook stove, which he smashed to flinters. There being no ladder at hand by which to return to the cell, and having no money to pay the damages, he concluded to "git," and he did. There were electrical disturbances in 1837, which as a boy attracted my attention. I allude to the magnificent thunder storms and vivid lightning. These storms were remarked upon at the time by others, and I think they have not since been equaled. My recollection has recently been confirmed by Giles C. Hard, of Guilford, Parson K. Johnson, of Mankato, Minn. and William Cunningham, of California.

A most conspicuous feature upon the prairie disappeared long ago. I have reference to the rings of dark, weedy vegetation about two feet high, and from ten to one hundred feet in diameter. These rings were plainly visible half a mile away and had nothing in common with the buffalo wallow of the western plains. The dark vegetation of the larger ones was from four to ten feet wide, with the inside of prairie grass, the earth as level as a floor, and the ring as true as though made with a compass. I never heard an explanation of the phenomenon except that lightning had struck there, until since I commenced to write these "Reminiscences," when "Lish"Kirk an old-timer who preceded me declared "the buffalo made 'em." (?) They were most common where the sod was underlaid by gravel, and on high, dry prairie, without method as to position, and universal throughout northern Illinois. There was a large buffalo wallow near the northeast corner of Second and Market streets,and a smaller one near the corner northeast from St. James church when I arrived.

Christian Frederic Charley("old Charley")was the first professional butcher to locate in Rockford. He was put ashore from a keel boat early in June, 1838, together with all the movable paraphernalia of his craft,containd in an immense ironbound chest. This boat was from the head waters of the Pekatonika (that's the way it was spelled in the "Rockford Star" in 1841,) bound for St. Louis, and loaded with lead and petries. The craft made one or more following trips the same year. Old Charley was a German and to the best of my recollection the first of that nationality to locate in Rockford. He was thoroughly versed in the mysteries of compounding bologna sausage,liverworts and the various strange edibles which his fellow countrymen have since made so popular. He built a slaughter house on the bank of the river on lot 3, block A, opposite the water works. set up his block in the basement of the Rockford house, and commenced business the same year.

Old Charley's slaughter house brings to mind while I write, a reminiscence of other parties who catered to the wants of the growing town and who in after years proved successful fishermen. The event and the fishing came off early in 1838 soon after the ice had gone out. There was a small bayou some twenty rods above State street in which the ice still remained. Goodyear A. Sanford and the late John Platt, had a seine which they operated for the benefit of the parties directly interested. They came over from the west side one morning, pushed the ice out from this bayou and about ten o'clock had the stream and bank clear for the first haul. By this time a number of the east siders had congregated on the bank, among them D. S. Haight, who, before it was made, bought the proceeds of the haul for five dollars, cash in advance. The reader will note, that even then, one of the parties transacted business in banking style. The haul was made, and sixty four black bass of magnificent proportions secured. Before the seine was ready for the next haul the assembly had increased in numbers, my father being among them and the market was bullish in the bidding for the next haul. After much chaffering my father secured it for seven fifty, spot cash before the boat pushed out. They got forty-two bass this time, like unto the first lot. The reason I remember so distinctly, is that Haight and my father pooled issues, and under his directions I dressed and salted the fish. By this time the market was excited, prices tended skyward, and "Gunlock" (Tom Miller,) bid ten dollars, stipulating the haul be made strictly as he should dictate. The result was a water haul, when Messrs. Sanford and Platt put the seine aboard the boat and returned to the west side.

Some twenty years ago I stated, and it was so published at the time in one of the local papers, that the first session of the circuit court, the Hon. Dan Stone presiding, was held in the Rockford House. A recent examination of the docket has convinced me I was mistaken. The first session of the court was held October 6, 1837, at the house of Daniel S. Haight, as the law provided and the docket states. The petit jurors in attendance were: Edward Cating, James B. Martyn, Joel Pike, William Pepper, Richard Montague, Isaac N. Cunningham, Thatcher Blake, Henry Thurston, Charles I. Horsman, David Goodrich, James Jackson and Cyrus C. Jenks. The judge appointed Seth B. Farwell prosecuting attorney *pro tem*. Through an oversight I omitted to copy the names of the grand jurors. It was the second session, 31st of May, 1838, I saw, which was quite largely attended and had both grand and petit juries. As I had never seen a court in session where a judge presided, I most distinctly remember my surprise to find the judge, the Hon. Dan Stone, occupying one of the few chairs we had in the house, while it was the jury who "sat upon the bench."

The first building erected for the use of courts, religious meetings, etc., was built by Daniel S. Haight in the summer of 1838, on the southeast corner of Market and Madison streets. Some of the lawyers who attended the early courts, in after years ranked among the most able men in the profession. I recall Judge Drummond and Thompson Campbell, of Galena; a Mr Joel Wells, who stumped the district for congress, N. B. Judd, of Chicago, and Seth B. Farwell and Martin P. Sweet, of Freeport. Of Thompson Campbell I am impelled to make more than a passing mention. As an orator, he was, by his friends, considered to be without a peer in the nation, even the fame of "the mill boy of the Slashes" paled in his presence. Sweet and Farwell were remarkably successful in their pleas before a jury, and for unique methods, humor and invective, Seth Farwell had no rival, Campbell and Farwell were sent to California by the government as commissioners to try the land titles which came up in relation to the Mexican land grants, and both died in that state.

The late Hon. John Wentworth made his maiden speech in Rockford, having volunteered his services as attorney in a case that promised to be game. Long John was as well known in this county as in his own district, possibly better, and he always came to Rockford while attending to the congressional fence repairing, a duty which he accomplished in the most thorough manner. The last time he ran for congress the convention was held at Dixon, and he came to Rockford with three four horse coaches loaded with his friends. In order that he might have altitude in which to stretch himself, he sat on the middle seat next the door with his head out of the window. As they were leaving town, Charley Tyler hailed him with, "Hello, John, where you're goin ?" To congress, by ——," and he did.

In May last, I wrote the Hon. R. R. Hitt at Washington for certain information from the Post Office Department, and a few days after, and before his reply could have been received, sent a second epistle to the effect that the task I had undertaken was greater and more difficult than I had anticipated. That neither my education, habits, or avocations in life had fitted me for an author. That I felt confident the statements I should make would in future years be accepted as authority, and taking a broad view of the situation, and also that the task was at best a thankless one, I was disposed to throw it up then and there. To this Mr. Hitt replied as per his letter of May 19th (here inserted), which together with encouragement from various old timers have induced me to proceed.

HOUSE OF REPRESENTATIVES, U. S. }
WASHINGTON, D. C., May 19, 1890. }

JOHN H. THURSTON, ESQ., 209 South Madison St., Rockford, Ill.

Dear Sir:—I have read your second letter of the 16th, with increasing interest, and trust you will not forget your promise to send me a copy when you print, for I have had a kindred feeling and experience. In that same year, 1837, on the 15th of September, I came, a little child, with our family, to Ogle county, and remember the incidents of the life during the "forties" with the photographic fidelity with which all events connected with our youth are impressed upon the memory. And there was, in fact, much more of individuality in the life of each one then, of freshness and hope and originality in the life of the community than in the uniformity that prevades today. With the growth of a great population, the events of each individual's life are dwarfed into pettiness and monotony. The insecurity of the earlier time gave a flavor of something akin to danger, The rapid changes in men's condition coming from an older and fixed community into the new and wilder region of the Rock River Valley were replete with many stirring incidents worthy of record. But in recording how things are reversed! Nowadays three to four columns a day are published of local details in a town. Then scarcely a word was printed in the whole community. Only from the letters, and scanty enough they are, of those who are gone, and from the reminiscences of old settlers like yourself, can we expect these souvenirs to be gathered up for permanent preservation. I hope you will not weary in your work. You will find as you talk with your cotemporaries of another time, memories awaken that will give you incidents that you had not thought of for long, and will learn others from them.

Very truly yours, R. R. HITT.

OFFICE OF THE POSTMASTER GENERAL, }
WASHINGTON, D. C., May 21, 1890. }

HON. R. R. HITT, House of Representatives:

Dear Sir:—I am in receipt of your letter of the 19th inst., asking for certain information in reference to the postoffices of Rockford, Rockton, Roscoe, Byron, and Oregon, Ill.; and of the time of the appointment of Mr. Daniel S. Haight as postmaster at Rockford.

In reply permit me to say that the records of the department are quite meager as to the offices during the early history of the service. I am able, however, to give you the following information:

ROCKFORD—Daniel S. Haight was appointed postmaster August 31, 1837, and served until June 26, 1840.

ROCKTON—This office was established as Pekatonica, and Mr. George Stevens was appointed postmaster December 26, 1838, and served until May 13, 1840. Sometime between that date and February 26, 1846, the name of the office was changed, and on the latter date Charles Kane was appointed postmaster.

ROSCOE—Was established as a special office and Mr. Ralph M. P. Abell was appointed postmaster July 26, 1837. He served until July 12, 1839.

BYRON—Was established as a special office May 26, 1838, and Asa G. Spalding was appointed postmaster.

OREGON—This office was then known as Oregon City. Mr. D. H. T. Moss was appointed postmaster May 15, 1837, and served until November 13, 1841.

Trusting this information may be of service to you and Mr. Thurston, I am, very truly,

J. W. WANAMAKER, *Postmaster General.*

As noted in the letter from the postmaster general, Daniel S. Haight was the first postmaster, his commission running from August 31, 1837, until June 26, 1840. The first mail arrived about September 15, 1837. Previous to this, the mail had been brought from Chicago by parties making the trip for supplies, an order upon the postmaster at that office for the mail being left at Haight's house, to which each man attached his name. The postage on letters from the east was twenty-five cents, and the time in transit from fifteen to thirty days. When the mail arrived there was no key and it went back unopened. At the second arrival a key had been provided, but Haight, who could not master the combination, turned it over to Giles C. Hard, his right hand man in emergencies, and who is entitled to whatever of honor and fame there may be in having opened the first mail in Rockford.

Haight built a small building in the summer of 1837, on the site of No. 107 South Madison street, for a post office, which was used until the following year, when he put up quite a commodious building on the site of No. 312 State street, with ante-room, boxes, etc. This structure was used for a post office during several following administrations. My father selected box 100; from him it went to Haight, and when he left the town in the winter of 1847-8, it was turned over to me, and was my box until the advent of free delivery.

The first theatrical exhibition in Rockford was given October 29, 1838 (I get the date from an old account book), in the Rockford House, by the troupe of the elder Jefferson, the father of "Joe" Jefferson, since become of world wide fame as an actor, more particularly so from his deliveration of "Rip Van Winkle." "Joe" was about ten years old at the time, and sang and acted "Lord Lovel," a new ballad then. The troupe were stranded here while en-route from Chicago to Galena, being unable to cross the river by heavy ice running in the stream. The last time he was here, "Joe" was interviewed by a reporter for one of the local papers, and he related his early visit to Rockford correctly, except he thought it was the Washington House where the troupe played.

CHAPTER V.

First Iron Foundry—First Dentist—"Doc" Webber, the Portait Painter—Whitney, the Thief—Broadies and Driscolls—Nigger Baby—"Duke" Wellington—Robbery of McKenney's Store as related by "Brad"—Brad's Full Dress Suit—He Makes Morning Calls—Robbery of William Mulford—Set There, You D——d Curly-Headed Irishman—Robbers and Pirates—Chain the Old Devil.

The first iron foundry was started, as near as can be ascertained, in 1841-2, by Peter H. Watson, but proved an abortive attempt owing to the charcoal fuel. The blast was produced by horse power. This Mr. Watson was at one time Assistant Secretary of War during the late unpleasantness, and at a later period President of the New York & Erie Railway. The foundry was located at about the centre of the east half of block 18, next south of the public square.

Since this paragraph was written Mr. Harvey H. Silsby, now residing at La Cygne, Linn county, Kansas, who came here from Acworth, New Hampshire, early in May. 1838, supplies me with items from which I compile a brief history of this pioneer foundry.

The original proprietors were Chandler & Watson, succeeded by Reynolds & Lyon; Lyon & Chamberlin; John Steves; Harvey H. Silsby; Loami Peake in 1850, and by him sold to James L. Fountain, who removed the apparatus to New Milford. Mr. Silsby thinks the foundry first started in 1842-3, and commenced to melt iron in what may be termed a pocket furnace, which was nothing more than a common blacksmith's forge, in which they melted about 100 lbs. at one heat, and which they sometimes charged five or six times a day. They afterwards put up a cupola furnace. This pocket furnace agrees with my recollection of the fixture. I was present at the first heat, as I distinctly remember the fuel was charcoal and the apparatus open on top. The largest portion of this first charge was not melted sufficiently to be made available. The bellows was after a plan of a steam engine; a piston, with a cylinder three feet in diameter and about the same length, with a receiver above, on which were weights to force a regular blast; the machine being worked by horse power. It appears that in 1844 they had got well started, as they were then building threshing machines and horse-powers with which to drive them. These machines were a failure, as they cut the grain.

During Mr. Silby's administration, (1847-8 to 1850) Lehigh coal, brought from Chicago, cost about $16.00 per ton; pig iron, $30.00 per ton. Patterns were furnished and castings sold for five cents per pound for ordinary work, while light castings brought seven to ten cents. The business was fairly profitable for the time under Mr. Silsby's supervision, as when he sold out in 1850 it realized about one thousand dollars per year.

As an instance of how slight an incident may sometimes change the direction of the energies of a man's life in the struggle for existence, and particularly as illustrative of a marked characteristic in the temperment of all pioneers; their desire for change and the ease and quickness with which they accomplished it, Mr. Silsby tells me, that at a week's notice in the spring of 1850, he had sold out this foundry and was off across the plains for California.

I think Jonathan T. Miller was the first dentist in the town who would be recognized by the profession, and his advent was about 1843, although he was here in 1841, and applied for a situation as teacher in the brick school house on the southeast corner of the public square. As some sort of a school fight was going on at the time, he withdrew his application and returned to New York state. There was, however, a tooth carpenter here in the fall of 1837, who had a rough experience. He whitened the boys' teeth and set false incisors, which he fastened to the old stump with a metal pin. I was watching his operations while he worked upon "Ike" Forshay, and when he struck the incisor a smart blow driving it into the old stump, "Ike" hauled off and knocked him over.

Ebenezer S. ("Doc") Webber, who came here from Niles, Michigan, in 1840, was the first portrait painter. His studio occupied the second floor of the brick part of the building now standing at No. 114 North Madison street. He delineated most of the boys about town on the east side, among them myself; the charge in my case being fifteen dollars, for which I had to hustle "right smart," and paid in installments of five dollars each.

Thieves, gamblers, and desperate characters were traversing the country, and Rockford appears to have been a conspicuous crossing point with the fraternity. I recall one fellow by the name of Whitney ranging from the Illinois river to Mineral Point, who made no pretense of being anything but a thief. An old timer relates an incident in Whitney's career which came off in the Rockford House. At breakfast, my father sat at the head of the table with Whitney upon one side and near him. Whitney asked if he intended the remark he had just made to apply to him? To this my father replied, "if the coat fits you may wear it." Whitney drew his pistol, leveled it, and at the same instant, two men sitting on the opposite side of the table drew pistols and covered Whitney, when he concluded the odds were against him and put up his weapon.

The Broadies and Driscolls, two families of thieves from Ogle county, were frequent visitors in the town, and usually brought with them a famous quarter horse called "Nigger Baby," offering to bet fabulous (at that time) sums, "the Nigger could beat any horse, mare, or gelding in the town," and he usually did if matched. The fame of the "Nigger" had extended in the fall of 1838 to central Indiana, and a horse was brought from that locality to get a race with him. A match was finally arranged at 600 yards, in which the "Nigger" gave his opponent fifty feet at the outcome. The contest came off on the Kishwaukee road half a mile south of the town, and the crowd exceeded all previous gatherings in the county. To the surprise of most of them, the "Nigger" was easily defeated.

From 1838 to '48 inclusive, Rockford was a regular stopping place for the Mississippi river card sharps, when they crossed the country from or to Chicago. They carried a perfect paraphernalia of gambling implements, roulette, faro layout, etc., in innocent looking traveling trunks. I recall one of the fraternity known as "Duke" Wellington, who in the winter of 1846-7 won $700 from Martin O. Walker, of the stage firm of Frink & Walker.

I am indebted to Bradford McKenney, now residing in Ogle county, near Daysville, for the following graphic account of the robbery of his brother William's grocery store in September, 1843. The building occupied the site of No. 818 East State street. The narrative is in "Brad's" own unique style, and will readily be recognized by all his old friends and acquaintances of "ye olden time." It is the first and only account of the details of the event which has ever been published.

While clerking for my brother William in his store at Rockford on the east side during the summer of 1843, I slept on the counter right over the money drawer. The money was kept in two trunks under the counter upon which I slept. One was a large strong trunk, and in that all the money that was not to be used for making change was put. On top of this one was a small one in which money needed for making change was put. No safe in Rockford at that time.

In the lower trunk, early in September, had accumulated about twelve hundred dollars, and as my brother had intended to go to New York the latter part of August, but had been delayed, he had made no effort to get exchange on New York. On the night of September 15th, about half past three, I was awakened by a noise under the counter where the trunks were, and the next instant something hit my feet and I raised up to find out what it was. The rain was pouring down in torrents; it was thundering fearfully, and a flash of lightning about every minute. I put my hand onto a trunk handle. Just then came a flash of lighting and I saw a man I took to be "Tut" Baker—I think his name was John—who I was well acquainted with, and says I, "what in —— are you doing here?" and says he, "keep still, Brad, it's all right." The moment I heard his voice I knew it was not "Tut" Baker, for I had known him ever since I had been in Rockford. " Bill sent me here to take these trunks and hide them, and then he can say he has been robbed, and can settle with his New York creditors and make a big thing out of it." "But," says I, "who the —— are you, anyhow?" "Oh!" says he, "it's all right. Bill understands it; you just keep still and it will be all right." "No," says I, "that won't go down, Bill don't owe anything in New York, and besides that I am —— —— sure that if there had been anything of that kind going on I should have heard of it before this time." "Now, Brad, I tell you Bill and I understand it and its all right." "Well" says I, "you can't have the trunk anyhow." Just then he gave the trunk a jerk, but I had got both hands hold of it and it didn't move easily. "Now look here" says he, "if you want to live, you just keep still and let go of that trunk; I ain't going to run all this risk for nothing." Just feel of that" said he, and I felt something touch me on my breast, and a flash of lightning showed me a bowie-knife about a foot long lying slanting across my breast. I shoved the knife away with my right hand. "Take care" said he, "or you'll cut your fingers." "Now I want the key —— —— quick." The key was in my pants at the foot of the bed on the counter, and the trunk was on top of them. I thought I would not let him get the key quite so easy. "If you get the key" I said, "you'll have to find Bill." "Well then" said he, "I'll take the trunk." "No you won't" I said, and I slid off the counter and gave the trunk a jerk and tried to pull it off the counter, but I could not do it, for he had hold of the other end, and was still behind the counter where he had found the trunks. The next I saw of him, he was on the counter with his right hand around the trunk and his bowie knife in his left hand. I could see him plainly every time it lightened and that was every few seconds. "Now look here" said he, "By ——, if you don't let go of that trunk in less than a minute, I will cut your hand loose from it." and his bowie-knife was not a great ways above my hand either.

I thought about the best thing I could do, was to let go, and I did. I went to the front door, the key was in the lock on the inside. I unlocked it, took out the key and put it in the lock on the outside and locked the door. I shall never forget the cold bath I took the moment I stepped outside, for the rain was coming down not in torrents, but in great sheets and I had nothing on but my shirt. Just as I got the door locked, the stage was coming up that little rise of ground nearly opposite the store, with the horses on the gallop. I ran out in the road and made frantic appeals to the driver to stop the stage and have the passengers help me. The horses kind of slacked up a little and I thought he was a going to stop, and I began yelling robbers and help! He put the whip on the horses and on he went, and on I went for the Rockford House. I don't think I ever made such time before or since. I got there ahead of the stage. There was a dim light in the bar-room, but no one there. The moment I got inside, I yelled help and robbers! and kept yelling as I made my way to my brother's room, which had always been at the head of the stairs; but when I began pounding on the door and calling him, the yell that came from that room could be heard farther than mine. It was a woman's!!

Then I came to a dead halt, but the next instant a flash of lightning showed me the chamber door and I opened that and yelled "Where is Bill McKenney's room?" As I had to repeat it several times, I began to think they were all dead; but finally Old Capin answered, "down stairs in the bed-room off from the parlor with Church," (Judge Selden M. Church.) He had changed his room a day or two before and had forgotten to tell me; so I made for the stairs and just as I struck them, Old Capin shouted "what in sheol has broke loose?" but I did not have a chance to answer, for in my hurry to get down, I stumbled and fell to the bottom, gathered myself up and made my way to my brother's room.

If electric lights had been in full operation them days, I probably should have offered an apology to the lady that was just going into the bar-room as I landed at the bottom of the stairs, for my lack of a full dress suit, but I didn't, I hadn't time, and did my level best to wake him up suddenly. I think the Judge will remember that call, and as soon as I had made him understand what had happened, he told where to go for help, and among the first he told me to call on, was Bill McDole and Charley Oliver. I made a number of calls on First street, but I did not go in, for I was not suitably dressed for making morning calls. When I got back to the store, there was fifteen or twenty men on the sidewalk and among them was Bill McDole and Charley Oliver. It was still raining, and some of the men had umbrellas and several had lanterns, but by the time I got dressed it had nearly stopped and it was getting daylight.

We found he had cut away the putty from around a pane of glass; turned the window fastening, raised the window and put a stick under it to hold it up. The back door was unbolted and stood wide open. Some of the men had started out with lanterns and as soon as it was light enough to see, the men started out in every direction. The trunk was soon found down in the brush west of old Bill Hamilton's house, which stood on the lot now occupied by John Spafford's warehouse (northwest corner Madison and Market streets.) It was brought to the store and there was eight dollars in silver in it. They were so close after him he did not have time to get it all out. During the day several dollars were found between where Peacock's brewery now stands and Henry Ellis' house, and in old Boswell's buckwheat field, two sovereigns and five or six dollars in silver. They tracked him by the money he lost nearly to the road running up the river, there they lost track of him.

The next spring, James Gilbert found sixty-two dollars only a few rods from where the trunk was found. It had apparently been stamped into the ground. I was not a little astonished when he came in with it in his hat and dumped it down on the counter, and told me to count it; for says he, "I think it belongs to Bill," and that was the general conclusion, so my brother kept it, and it was all he ever got back.

Why I mention McDole and Oliver, is that at the time of the robbery, my brother considered them among his best friends, and in the Mulford trial it came out that they got up the sight and sent for another man to do the job, and that Bill McDole was at the back door while the fellow was in the store.

My brother had such confidence in them both as friends, that he would not believe they had anything to do with robbing him until he heard the testimony, and at the close of the trial, Bill McDole asked my father and brother both, to sign a bail bond right in the court house, but they told him the evidence was a little too strong.

Some have written accounts of that robbery in which they say I used a revolver, but I had no revolver, and up to that time had never seen a pistol, and I don't think the idea of being robbed ever came into my brother's head; I know it did not into mine. He never so much as mentioned it to me. There were no blinds on the front or back windows; only a paper curtain, and half the time I did not pull them down. BRADFORD MCKENNEY.

Saturday evening, November 9, 1844, William Mulford, residing on his farm in Guilford, four and one-half miles east on the Cherry Valley road, was robbed of five hundred dollars in money. He came to Rockford early the next morning, the writer meeting him on the steps of the Washington House, and was the first person to whom he mentioned the fact. I aroused Haight, Grant B. Udell a lawyer, James Mitchell clerk of the Circuit Court, with several others whose names I do not now recall, and we all went into Udell's office where Mr. Mulford related the events of the previous evening. Mr. James Mitchell was a large tall man, and while telling the story, Mr. Mulford believed at the time, as he afterwards told me, that Mitchell was the man who held his (Mulford's) own rifle, with the muzzle pressed against his back, as he forced him to precede him about the cabin while searching the premises, and he said he knew it would explode when the trigger was pulled. By this the reader may get some insight of the condition of society in a part of the "early days in Rockford," when an innocent man and estimable citizen as Mr. Mitchell was, may be temporarilly suspected of consorting with robbers, merely from his personal appearance. Mr. Mitchell went from Rockford to Freeport, where he resided until his death, about ten years ago.

From my personal knowledge of Mr. Mulford's character and bodily vigor, I have no hesitation in pronouncing him a game man, and if he could have secured his rifle, one at least of the robbers, would have been killed.

The following interesting details of what transpired that evening in the cabin, are supplied by his son Edward Mulford, who remarked when he handed me the notes from which I gather the account of the fracas, "I was there, but not much help, as I was six months old at the time."

In the fall of 1844, a well dressed man called at the house of William Mulford in the township of Guilford, four and one-half miles east of Rockford, and asked for employment, introducing himself as Mr. Haines. He staid but a few moments, and said as he departed that he would call again in a few days. Shortly after this one evening about nine o'clock, three masked men armed with pistols, knives and hickory clubs, came to the door of Mr. Mulford's house and knocked for admittance. John Carman, who was working for Mr. Mulford at the time, opened the door. As soon as the door was opened, one of the men grabbed Carman by the throat, backed him into the house and forced him down onto a vinegar barrel that was in the room, saying to him "set there, you d—d curly-headed Irishman." Mr. Mulford was in the room, and hearing some noise and scuffling, thought it was made by some of the neighboring boys, had paid no attention to it until he heard the order to Carman to sit down; that attracting his attention he looked around, and as he did so, asked "what is the racket here?" At this query, one of the gang stepped up to him and introduced himself and companions in the following words: "We are robbers and pirates from the upper seas. We are after your money, and by —— we will have it, and the best thing you can do is to let us have the money and be quiet; if you do not, we shall search for it."

Mr. Mulford told them he "had but little money, and none for them." The leader then ordered Mulford to be seated and they would commence the search. He stationed one of his men at the inside door armed with two pistols, several knives and a hickory club. Taking the candle from the table he cut it into three pieces, lighted them, placing one in each of the two windows, retaining the third piece for his own use in the search. They commenced at the bureau, taking every article out of the drawers, unfolding and carefully shaking them in order to discover any hidden treasure. Mrs. Mulford, who with her two children was lying on the bed, seeing them scatter and trample her clothing under foot, told them there was no money there, and having recognized the leader said to him, "Mr. Haines, you conduct yourself very differently from what you did the day you came to obtain employment." She had recognized him notwithstanding his disguise. Upon hearing this the robber drew a large knife from his belt and rushing to the bedside, said "Shut your —— clack, or I will leave a stain on the floor that will remain for ages." He then turned to his comrades and said, "Boys, I am known; I must make tracks." After they had looked over everything in the bureau they went upstairs. The first thing they came in contact with there, was a trunk belonging to John Saylor who worked for Mr. Mulford, but happened to be away that night. They took everything of value in the trunk and searched every nook and corner; finding nothing more worth taking, they came down and went into the cellar. The cellar was not stoned up, and rats had made several holes in the walls of earth. These holes they dug into with their knives to see if gold had been secreted there. They also cut open some pumpkins and turnips lying there, thinking gold might be concealed in the vegetables. There were a number of cakes of tallow in the cellar which they cut to pieces, saying "they had known women cunning enough to run tallow around gold.

Finding nothing of value in the cellar they returned to the place where they commenced, and talked over the disappointment. While they were conversing, one of them discovered three small drawers at the top of the bureau which they had over looked in their first search, and asked for the keys. Mr. Mulford told them the last recollection he had of them, they were in the stable behind the horses. They said they did not like to take the top off the bureau and would go and get them, so two of them went to the stable for the keys. Mr. Mulford thought that by getting some of the party out of the house, he might succeed by moving carefully about in securing his rifle that was hanging under some clothing at one end of the room. After the men who had gone for the keys had left the house he got up and walked the floor, finally halting in front of the weapon and had just got his hand on the arm, when he heard a slight noise and looking over his shoulder saw the man who had been stationed at the door, standing behind him holding a pistol close to his head. This man then took the rifle and a shot gun that was hanging there and every moment after that while they remained in the house, held the rifle aimed at Mr. Mulford's head, so that if he attempted to get possession of any other weapon he would be prepared for him. The men could not find the keys in the stable and returned to the house very angry, and making many threats, swearing they would "chain the old devil, set the house on fire, and by the time he got well scorched he would tell where the keys were." As they said this, one of them ran his hand into his pocket, and Mrs. Mulford thought she heard something rattle like a chain: she then told them where the keys were. They soon unlocked the drawers and in one of them found five hundred dollars. It was in an envelope just as it was taken from the bank. The man Haines (Robert Burke) took it to the table and counted it, saying "three hundred and fifty dollars—this is worse than a wolf hunt." When Haines said "three hundred and fifty dollars," Mr. Mulford spoke up and said, "I do not wish to have you cheat your comrades, there is five hundred dollars in that package, and I should like to have you leave enough of it to pay my hired men who are poor." They said they intended to divide with him, but did not do so. They talked together for a few moments and then left the place.

Before leaving they asked Mr. Mulford what he intended to do? Cautioned him not to try and catch them as they were strong in numbers, and warned him several times not to go out of his house before daylight, as they would leave men stationed at the door, and if any living thing made its appearance outside of the door before daylight, it would be a corpse. They then a bade him good night, going out of the house backwards, with their guns and pistols pointed at Mr. Mulford as long as they could see him. It was ascertained afterwards, that two men were outside armed with rifles, and that was the reason why candles were placed at the windows.

CHAPTER VI.

First Tinner—Leach & Penfield—A Varied Assortment of Hardware—Willard Wheeler—A Deacons Decision on Shoemaker Loo and Division Loo—Doc. Searles He Builds the First Soda Fountain and A Rotary Steam Engine—Judge Blackstone's Experience with this Engine.—Laomi Peake Sen - Makes the First Harness—Value of Real Estate in 1839—Been Whipped a Thousand Times- First Brick Store on the East Side—First Cabinet Maker—An Early Subscription Paper—First Doctor—Old Froth—I've Killed More than Forty.--First Grist Mill—First Saloon—Tobacco Famine—Julius P. Bolivar MacCabe—First Religious Services—First Quarterly Meeting—First Camp Meeting—First Religious Society—Thousand Legs and His Jack.

I have been unable to ascertain the name of the first tinner in Rockford, but I do recollect that he was here in the early fall of 1838, and in the employ of Leach & Penfield (Shepherd Leach and David S. Penfield. Mr. Penfield was a native of Pittsfield, Vt.), whose store occupied the site of No. 322 east State street, and was erected by Tinker & Johnson. I recall his presence in the town at that early day, from an incident personal to myself. In the fall of 1838 a stove was required to be set up in the dining room of the Rockford House, and as my father was confined to his bed in the adjoining room by rheumatism, I was detailed for the job. The pipe was irregular in size, and required some thirty feet in length to reach the chimney. The old gentleman was irritable and lay on his couch blowing me up for my inability to perform the task. I too, was "blowing" in subduced tones (but none the less emphatic on that account,) the whole outfit. Finally the services of this tinner were secured, and the majority of mankind will agree in the conviction, that the man who under like conditions, can place thirty feet of horizontal stove pipe in position without swearing, is indeed an artist in his line.

Mrs. D. S. Penfield informs me, the stock of Leach & Penfield would invoice about three thousand dollars, and contained a general assortment of merchandise; iron, tin, and woodenware, groceries, dry goods, millinery and fancy goods, etc.

Willard Wheeler, who came here from St. Thomas, Upper Canada, in September 1839, was the second tinner in the town, and as he continued the business for several years afterwards, it has generally been supposed he was the first in that line. His peculiarities will be remembered by all his friends and associates. His thorough and practical knowledge of the games and pastimes then in vogue, may not have been suspected by his brethren in the church. In the early forties, a dispute occurred at a gambling table and the decision was left to "Doc" Searles. The legality of his ruling was disputed, and it was finally agreed that the question be submitted to Willard Wheeler, whose decision should be final, and that "Doc" himself should state the matter in dispute. Willard (who at one time was, and could then have been a bad man in a row,) decided that in shoemaker loo and division loo, the "Doc" had decided correctly, by both law and precedent.

Any account of "Early Days in Rockford," and the prominent characters in the town at the time, would most certainly be incomplete, should it fail to mention Hosea D. ("Doc") Searles, who came here from his native state of Connecticut in the early summer of 1841, and who almost immediately acquired the sobriquet of "Dogbutton," the seed of a vegetable from which strychnine is extracted, with one of which he attempted to "ante" at a game of brag. This title was however, soon dropped, and subsequently he was universally known as "Doc" from his profession as a druggist. He was the founder (I think in 1842) of the drug business now carried on by the sons of the late William Worthington at No. 422 east State street, the firm being Searles & Worthington. He possessed a fund of dry humor that was unique in its character, and which to the gratification of "the boys," was frequently brought into requisition during the long evenings in winter, the "Doc" relating some humorous incident which had recently transpired, and wherein one of "the boys" then present was a factor, his own face as calm as a summer morning, while the audience was convulsed with laughter.

He possessed mechanical skill of a high order. He built and put in operation the first soda fountain in Rockford, the design of the machine being his own—it was built of wood—and he constructed and put it together in person. I am unable to describe the apparatus, except that it had a wooden lever about ten feet long, and squirted like a fire engine while filling the glasses, the said "glasses," as a rule, having had "a stick in 'em" before being filled with soda water. He built a rotary steam engine, which he sold to the Mt. Morris Seminary. This machine was also his own design and construction, with the exception of the boiler, which was of copper and supplied by Williard Wheeler.

This engine was the cause of a ludicrous incident that will be fully appreciated by those still here who knew "Judge" Blackstone. The machine set in a frame the width of a counter and about three feet long; when in operation it was placed in the center of the store on the counter that we might get a better view. The steam escaped through the spokes of a wheel some twelve inches in diameter and when in operation, was slightly enveloped in vapor. The boiler was filled with water, the fire started and the engine ran while the supply lasted, there being no pump to the apparatus. The first time it was started for exhibition to the general public was in the drug store, and the room was crowded, the "Judge" being in the front rank, as he always tried to be for that matter. There was a high pressure of steam and a small chip in the water had been forced into the safety valve of the boiler. The steam instantly escaped with an unearthly scream like unto a whistle, which none of us had ever heard before. We all bolted for the door except the "Doc," whose attainments told him the thing wasn't going to "bust" under the conditions. Among the first to leave was the "Judge;" in the fracas he was knocked down and the crowd behind went over his prostrate body, myself being among the first to tread on him. The volume of oaths, imprecations and invectives that came from the "Judge" while he was on the floor, was unprecedented even in his career and he was the most original character in that line in the state. When the "Judge" finally got upon his feet, the room was clear, the machine was running smoothly and the "Doc" in his most suave tone and manner inquired, "Judge, what is the matter?"

"Matter enough, by ——. A small man has no chance at all in this crowd."

In the summer of 1851, the "Doc" Andrew Brown and myself made a trip to Chicago. In the center of Garden Prairie, standing in a cornfield, we saw the "Pioneer," the first locomotive in use by the Galena and Chicago Union Rail Road. "Andrew," said "Doc," "do you see that hoss? Let's go and look at her." While examining the machine, "Doc" remarked to me, "John, I can make a machine like that," and he did. This machine ran on a circular track three feet in diameter, the propelling force being a spirit lamp. When once started there was no way of stopping it while the lamp burned and the water lasted, and it whizzed around the track after the fashion that Mark Beaubein kept tavern. His only failure in a mechanical way of which I have any knowledge, was an attempt to manufacture a Chinese gong. I went with him one cold day in winter to N. B. Gaston's scale works in Beloit, where he melted his compound of metals in a crucible. The casting was a failure, and he remarked to me, "John, the mould must be hot."

I am indebted to Mr. and Mrs. Laomi Peake Senior for the following account of the first harness maker in Rockford. Mr. Peake, who is a native of Salisbury, Herkimer county, New York, emigrated from St. Thomas, Upper Canada, to Rockford, in September, 1839, being one of the few among the early arrivals who possessed capital, having about five thousand dollars in money. His family arrived April 15, 1840. There was a harness maker here before he arrived, so Mr. Peake informs me, who did not remain long, and who made repairs only. Of this man I have no recollection, neither have I found a person who does remember him. As Mr. Peake was the first person who made a harness here, and carried on the business for many years subsequently, he may claim to have been the first in that line.

Mr. Peake bought the lot on the northeast corner of First and State streets, 66 feet on First street by 156 feet on State street for one hundred dollars, and put up a brick building 22 by 35 feet, with two stories and basement, at a cost of fifteen hundred dollars, immediately after his arrival. The corner of this lot is now occupied by the Manufacturers' Nat. Bank. In the summer of 1852, he completed the brick block now standing on the corner of this lot at a cost of about $7,000, with an additional expense of $1,000, in fitting up the hall which occupied the whole of the third floor. The same year of his arrival he purchased for a farm, a tract of one hundred and thirty acres on State street, for which he paid $750. The southwest corner of this land was at or near Summit street, extending east to Prospect street on East State street. Peake's block (corner State and First streets) was burned November 27th, 1857, the side and rear walls remaining. The corner store at the time of the fire was occupied by Huntington & Barnes (C. A. Huntington and Robert Barnes) for a book store, at a rental of $450 per year for the room, with $80 additional for a room on the second floor in which they operated a ruling machine. Kirk & Haines, the present owners, purchased the property in the fall of 1858 for $4,000, and rebuilt the block the following year. I have given these particulars in order that a knowledge of the value of landed property at the time may be recorded.

The beauty of the landscape looking south from the top of the hill on east State street, before it was disfigured by improvements, was as well known and appreciated in the forties as it has ever been since. "Judge" Blackstone used to relate an anecdote of one of the teamsters, who with six horses freighted merchandise from Galena to Chicago. One lovely day in summer, he halted the team to breathe on the brow of the hill. That he had a genuine love in his honest heart for the beautiful in nature as he gazed over the magnificent panorama of waving grain spread out before him, was evident when he turned to his companion exclaiming, "Well Bill, by ——; I've lived in nineteen states and three territories, been whipped a thousand times, but I'm damned if I ever see so pretty a country as that."

The first brick store on the east side occupied the site of No. 113 South Madison street, and was built by Descombe Simons ("Buck" Simons) in the summer of 1839. It was a two-story and basement building about 23x30 feet in size, and was taken down in 1887.

Thomas Johnson, an Englishman, was the first cabinet maker in Rockford. He came here from New York city where he had worked at his trade for several years. On the trip west, he fell in company with William Peters, John Beattie, D. D. Alling and G. A. Sanford, the party arriving in Rockford early in the season of 1837. After making his claim on the "south branch," he set up his bench in one of the basement rooms of the Rockford House. In the opinion of those among the early settlers who still possess some of his furniture, a more accomplished workman has never handled a tool in Rockford. He made two eight square ottomans (we had no chairs) for my mother in the winter of 1837-8, that are as sound to-day as when they first left his hands. Mr. Johnson made the first musical instrument constructed in Rockford. I have the original subscription paper for the article, which is in the handwriting of my father, and herewith present a copy, *verbatim et literatim* of the document, so far as may be done with type.

"We the undersigned, agree to pay the several sums annexed to our Respective names for the purtchs (sic) of a bass Drum for the use and accommodation of the village of East Rockford to be subject to the controle (sic) of a Certain number of Trustees to be chosen by those who are proprietors in the Instrument.

ROCKFORD, AUGUST 6TH, 1838.

pd Henry Thurston	$2	00
pd Daniel S Haight	3	00
pd S C George	1	00
pd Daniel Halsey	1	00
pd John B Clark	1	00
pd Thomas Miller	1	00
James B Martyn	1	00
pd L & W Bundy	1	00
pd James T Taylor		25
Harmon Loomis	1	00
Pd Little & Bockus	1	00
Col J L White		50
John C Kemble	1	00
P Alexander H Miller		50
Harvey W Bundy	1	00
pd F C Walker		50
Doct Goodridgh	1	50

It will be observed some of the subscribers were "dead heads," as has proved the case under like circumstances in after years. Inclosed with the subscription list was the following bill made out in a different handwriting:

AUGUST 6, 1836. (?)

to 1 Drum	$12	00
4 Bunches cord	1	00
2 hundyd (sic) Brass nails		25
1 bunch tacks	0	8
1 pair of drum sticks	0	50
to Lumber for drum	1	62¼
Straps for drum	1	88
to 1 doz of scruws (sic)		37½
1 paint brush		18¼
to 1 thoushand (sic) of tacks		12¼
to 1 drum hook	1	00
	19	01¼

Rec'd of Henry Thurston payment in full of above bill." The receipt of payment is written in pencil and is indistinct. Mr. Johnson went to California in 1862, as near I can ascertain, and returned once since then for a short visit with his old friends. The drum itself, went the way destined for all bass drums. When Haight left the town he turned it over to me. Shortly after I loaned it for some festival at Twelve Mile Grove, and in the fracas a wagon pole demolished it.

Levi Moulthrop, the dry goods merchant on the west side, supplies me with the following facts relating to his father: "Levi Moulthrop, M. D., was the first practicing physician in Winnebago county. He was born at Litchfield, Conn., Nov. 1st, 1805, and attended school there during his boyhood. Later on he studied medicine and graduated from Fairfield College, New York, January 23, 1834. The following winter he migrated west, locating at Ottaway, Illinois, December 1, 1834, where he commenced the practice of his profession. The wonderful beauty and many advantages of the Rock River Valley were then being heralded far and wide, influencing Doctor Moulthrop to make the trip on horseback in the autumn of 1835 to this county, where he purchased a claim of several hundred acres in what is now the town of New Milford. June 30, 1840, he was married to Margaret, eldest daughter of Sampson and Ann George, from Yorkshire, England, who with their family arrived at Rockford in the autumn of 1836. Doctor Moulthrop died September 12, 1840."

Among the skilled physicians who were here at an early day, Doctor Josiah C. Goodhue should, and did then, occupy a prominent position. He was not only skilled in his profession as then practiced, but his knowledge had a wide range, and his intellectual strength enabled him to grapple with any subject or opponent that might for the occasion be present. He was a teetotaler in those days of the universal use of strong drink, but chewed tobacco immoderately, which habit caused the boys to promptly dub him "Old Froth," a title by the way they were wise enough not to apply in his presence. He was a fluent extemporaneous speaker, and few indeed there were who could compete with him in argument. It was his delight to draw out the opinions of others, and regardless of his own convictions upon the subject, take the opposite side of the question. He was a skilled chess player. most urbane and gentle in his manner when the occasion should demand, and quite otherwise when the time and the patient would require an opposite style. He never would admit his patients were sick. When called to prescribe for some rough character, he would look at the patient for a moment, note the pulse and symptoms, and address him something after this fashion. "Sick, you're not half so sick as you will be. You d—m fool, why did you send for me ?"

A story was current, and from a personal knowledge of both the M. D's, I have no doubt is authentic, which ran something like this : Doctor —— heard that Doct. Goodhue had said that he, Doctor —— had killed Smith's child ; so he called to see and question him in relation to the rumor. Doct. Goodhue saw him coming and surmising what his errand might be, met him at the door with his most cordial urbane manner. "I am very glad indeed to see you sir—come in." This warm reception rather abashed Doctor ——, but he went in and stated his errand, saying, "Doctor Goodhue, I hear you have said that I killed Smith's child." Doct. Goodhue promptly interrupted him, saying, "Haven't you killed more than one ? Lord, I've killed more than forty ! If you haven't killed more than one you are no doctor at all ! ! !"

Some one said to him that he could not give up the use of tobacco, whereupon he threw away his cud, and for twelve months never put a particle of the weed in his mouth, when he again commenced its use saying he "knew it was good all the time." His death resulted from an accident brought about by the character of the man. He could not, and would not be dictated to, or ordered by any person. He was called to prescribe for some of the family of the late Richard Styles, four miles west on the State road. After caring for the patient he accompanied Mrs. Stoughton to her home, but a few rods away on the opposite side of the road. When they got inside the gate—it was a dark night—she told him they were digging a well in the yard, and to remain where she had placed him until she returned with a light. Before she could get back, he had fallen into the excavation. He was taken out as soon as possible and revived sufficiently to ask what had happened. When told, he replied it would be fatal. Peace to his ashes. To the writer he was ever most kind.

Col. James Sayre, who migrated from New Jersey to Juliet (now Joliet) in the 30's, came to Newburg in the spring of 1835 and erected a grist mill there, the first in the county, which began to grind early in the winter of 1837-8. I went there with a bushel of wheat on my pony the third day after the machinery started. There was no bolting apparatus at the time and the meal was sifted by hand. My recollection is the machinery was crude and the site as a mill, was abandoned soon afterward.

Samuel ("Sam") Little, an Englishman, opened the first bar (saloon) in June, 1837, on the spot now occupied for the same business by Fritz Spahr, at 316, East State street. He built a small one-story building, the length of the longest piece of siding to be obtained at Kent's mill. This building fronted west, but he afterwards turned it to front on State street. For the majority of years since this site was first occupied, it has been used for the sale of liquor. I speak from personal knowledge in stating that there has never been a business day in Rockford since the 12th day of March, 1837, when a glass of liquor could not be purchased in the town. I also state upon the same authority that nine hundred ninety-six (996) barrels of whisky were sold in 1857, from the store now standing at No. 314 east State street.

Since the introduction of King Gambrinus, the consumption of strong liquors in proportion to the population in the city has decreased largely. In the early 60s, in company with others one warm afternoon, I was in Schicker's basement, The beer was cool, we were hungry and the pretzels appetizing. Among those present was "Joe" Schmauss the elder. "Joe," said I, "how much beer can you drink and not become intoxicated; just enough to feel good?" "Well, I don't know, Mr. Thurston, but I think about forty glasses!!"

For six weeks during the winter of 1837-8 there was no tobacco for sale in the town, and the discarded quids were carefully laid aside to dry for smoking. Great was the joy when word came that J. C. & C. Waterman had opened a store at Newburg, supplied with an abundant stock of the weed. The boys "chipped in" and despatched one of their number for a supply, his contribution to the fund being doing the errand. In less than three hours after his departure, "Old Hays" was descried by anxious eyes approaching the town, his horse on a smart gallop, and holding an immense plug of tobacco in each hand, with which he belabored the animal as he rode through and around the starving crowd. The supply having been divided, "Old Hayes" collected his tithe, and when the circuit was completed, had more tobacco than any three of them.

Early in the winter of 1845, an eccentric genius who signed his autograph "Julius P. Bolivar McCabe," made his advent into Rockford and for the time being domiciled at the Washington House, "Judge" E. S. Blackstone, proprietor, which was also my abiding place. MacCabe had a genius for collecting statistics and compiled a census of the town which may be relied upon as correct in all the statements made. He was a dissipated character and thorough deadbeat, finally becoming so disagreeable, that at the united request of the boys as well as the earnest solicitation of "Judge" Blackstone, who could not turn him out of the house to perish, I drove him to Beloit and left him in the bar room of the tavern there.

MacCabe claimed to be a profound mathematician and set sums for myself and other youngsters. He told us to multiply 20£ by 20£. That problem being solved, he required we should multiply 19£, 19s, 11p 3f by 19£, 19s, 11p, 3f, and when we produced an aggregate approximating to the English national debt, confoundod us by referring to our solution of the first example. I think Judge S. M. Church may remember how anxiously we appealed to him for aid by which to get ahead of Mac.

The evening of August 6, 1882, the Rev. G. R. Van Horn, at the Centennial church, preached an historical discourse on "The Growth of Methodism in Rockford," which was afterwards published in the *Gazette*, and from which I make the following extracts: The reference to the organization of the first religious society in the county, is precisely as I remember a statement made by the late Samuel Gregory at a camp meeting in 1840.

"In the *Rockford Forum*," published by Austin Colton, of December 3, 1845, appears a well written article of historical value, from the pen of Julius P. Bolivar MacCabe, in which he makes the following statement:

The first religious services held by a white congregation in Winnebago county, were held in a log house belonging to Germanicus Kent, at Rockford in June 1835. Rev. Aratus Kent a Presbyterian clergyman of Galena, was the preacher and the families of Messrs Daniel S. Haight and Germanicus Kent 17 in number, then constituting all the white inhabitants except Mr. Stephen Mack were present.

"Methodism was introduced in the following year. In July 1836, William Royal preached in the house of Henry Enoch, seven miles northeast of Rockford." My recollection of Mr. Samuel Gregory's remarks in 1840, are that a party of five persons went from his home to Mr. Enoch's cabin in a wagon drawn by oxen, and he gave the route they pursued which was a short distance east of the spot where he then stood. (J. H. T.) "Mr. Royal was then in charge of the Fox River mission and traveled over a circuit which embraced twenty-eight preaching places. On his return to attend the annual conference which met at Springfield he passed through Rockford and on the second day of September 1836, he preached in the log house of Samuel Gregory, which stood then on what is now block 14 in Woodruff's second addition to Rockford. Ninth street bounding it on the west,

Eighth avenue on the south. At the close of his sermon he organized the first Methodist class, comprising five persons, namely: Samuel Gregory, Joanna Gregory, Mary Enoch, Daniel Beers and Mary Beers. Samuel Gregory was appointed leader." * * * * *

* * * * * * * * *

The first quarterly meeting ever held in Rockford was held late in the summer of this year (1838), in a barn belonging to Daniel S. Haight, and the barn was located south of State street, between Second and Third streets, facing east." (This is a mistake. It is the same barn I mention in my description of the town when I arrived and faced north and south. Haight sold it to Frink & Walker who moved it to the locality where it stood when the conference occupied it, and then faced east and west, and was being finished by its new owners for a stage barn. J. H. T.) "The frame of that barn was bought some years afterwards by Isaac Rowley and removed two miles east, where it was set up and enclosed, and where it stands to this day; its oaken timbers still sound as the doctrines preached within it during that meeting."

The first camp meeting in this county was held in the summer of 1840, on ground then belonging to Daniel Beers, on Pike Creek, probably a mile north of the Turner place on the State road; Nathan Jewett presiding elder. I was there three days, and most of the time for four nights. It was there where I heard Mr. Samuel Gregory make the statement of the first organization of the Methodist church in the county. The attendance was large, particularly so on Sunday, when a much larger audience was assembled than had ever before met in the county.

In my scrap book I find a clipping from the *Rockford Journal* of January 7, 1876, (which is here appended) of which the late Hiram R. Enoch was editor, and as he writes from personal knowledge, it may be accepted as authentic, regarding the early history of the Methodist church in Winnebago county.

"Historicus" of the *Gazette* has commenced correcting errors in the published chapters of his history of Winnebago county. If "Historicus" stops to correct all the errors he has made in his history, he will not get along very fast. One error in a recent chapter was so glaring that it is hardly worth while to correct it, yet we will do so. He said "the first Methodist sermons were preached in 1838 in the house of Mr. Boswell on the east side of the river." Now the fact is, the first Methodist sermon in the county was delivered in June, 1836, in the house of Henry Enoch, 7½ miles from Rockford, in what is now the town of Guilford. The first M. E. society in Winnebago county was also organized there in 1836, with five members; this membership being Daniel Beers and wife, Samuel Gregory and wife, and Mrs.

Henry Enoch, mother of the writer, and A. I. Enoch. This society was the organization on which the First M. E. church of Rockford was afterwards based. "Historicus" should brush up a little or his history will not be any more reliable "than last year's almanac."

Quite a noted character in his day and time, known by the sobriquet of "Thousand Legs," was Jonathan Weldon, of Westfield, the grandfather of the person of the same surname now residing there, and intimately connected with "Heaven," (?) who was recently delivered of a female child, as that community assert from immaculate conception. He was among the first settlers in the county, and I think had located in Westfield before I arrived. It was a current story in early days that Richard Montague said he left New Hampshire, not only to better his condition, but also in the pleasing belief that he had succeeded in getting away for all time from the locality infested by Jonathan Weldon. To his utter disgust, almost the first person he encountered when he arrived at Rockford was "Thousand Legs." His sobriquet originated from personal deformity of his legs, and to the best of my knowledge his wife, whom I never saw, was deformed like unto her husband, but worse. In short the couple were such as well informed people unite in the belief should not be allowed to propagate the species. His appearance as he swung along the trail on his crutches, and he could only do so for a short distance, was a sight to be avoided by hysterical females. His head, arms and body were large and muscular, and his appearance from his waist up, was as depicted of John the Baptist. The man was intellectual and shrewd. In one instance, single and alone, he successfully opposed the entire bar of the county in a case where a road was proposed to be laid through his land, the judge deciding there was not a legal road in the county. He was the cause of constant strife and turmoil in his neighborhood, and one dark night was taken from his house by a disguised party and carried out on the prairie, where they made preparations as he believed at the time, to hang him; but after a consultation took him to a school house and left him in the fire place covered with tar and feathers. He was the only man I ever met, who when casually about the house when dinner was to be served, whom Henry Thurston did not invite to dine with him. Thousand Legs and myself fell out at an early day, and from his manner in after years, I am confident he never forgot the incident. In the winter of 1839-40, I was crossing the river on the ice afoot, and at the east shore found him sitting in a jumper with the shafts broken, and unable to help himself. Two sleighs had passed him while I was on the ice, both leaving him to get out of the difficulty as best he could. He appealed to me for assistance, and I went to my sister's house and got a clothes line which

I had bought and given her a few days previously from my pocket money—coin of the realm being a scarce commodity—and tied the shafts of the jumper so as to enable him to drive up the hill while I walked beside the vehicle and halted him in front of Potter & Preston's store, telling him to go into the store and get a rope as I wanted that one. "To whom my good lad does this bit of cord belong?" "I bought it for my sister, Mrs. Shaler." "Ah! I see Mr. Shaler in front of the postoffice, I will mention it to him," and he immediately started and drove to the office. "Good afternoon Mr. Shaler, I trust thee and thy young wife are in the possession of sound health this beautiful winter day. Thee can see my jumper has met with a slight disaster. The lad informs me the cord which enabled me to get up the hill belongs to thee, and if thee will allow me to retain such as may be required, my ready hands will repair"—"Certainly, most certainly, Mr. Weldon, you are entirely welcome to the line." "No," I broke in, "you d—d old cuss; that cord is mine," and I rapidly untied and took it off, leaving him in the condition in which I found him, to the intense amusement of the bystanders.

Thousand Legs carried on his farm quite as successfully as the majority of the settlers, notwithstanding the deficiency in his means of locomotion. He was among the first in the county to raise mules, and nearly fifty years ago had in his possession a large Spanish Jack, gentle and kind in harness, which he sometimes drove to town. If there are any of the whigs or democrats of 1842 still remaining in Rockford, they may recall an episode in which John Bierer, a young lawyer, Thousand Legs, and the jack particularly, were prominent. One pleasant day in Autumn, an assembly of some fifty people had gathered on the northeast corner of State and Madison streets, in front of the Rockford House. There were no buildings on the west half of that lot at the time, and John Bierer, who had been sent out from near Pittsburgh, Pa., to "grow up with the country" mounted a dry goods box placed at a convenient place on this open space, and began addressing the audience upon the advantages of a home market—a la McKinley. Bierer was in full view of both the Rockford and Washington houses, and the loungers of the two hostelries were speedily congregated on the front steps. Among others who had been attracted to the spot was Jonathan Weldon, who with this jack hitched in the shafts of the wagon in which he sat, was in front of the Rockford house facing south. As Bierer got well warmed up on his subject he was in the midst of a flight of rhetoric, when the jack lifted his head and tail and saluted with a voice like a fog-horn—hee haw! hee haw!! hee haw!!! Bierer maintained his composure, waited until the animal had ceased; made some pleasant allusion to the incident and went on with his speech. A few moments later when the effect of the concert had partially subsided, the jack again lifted his voice, this time with increased volume, his head and tail vibrating perpendicularly as the volume of sound rose and fell. Hee haw! hee haw!! hee haw!!! came from his lungs with the blare of a thousand trumpets, when some person thrust a shingle profusely ornamented with tacks, under the root of his caudal appendage, and away went the jack with Thousand Legs behind him, down the trail to the ford, disappearing in a cloud of dust. There was no more political speaking that day, but the way the politicians "set 'em up" was a caution.

CHAPTER VII.

The Cold Winter of 1842-3—Two Feet of Snow April 1st, 1843—Pork Seventy-Five Cents per 100 lbs.—Deer Killed With Clubs—The Belle of the Jumper—Girls Have One Dress—Boys One Suit—Candy Pulls, Quiltings and Fandangos—Wheat Three Shillings per Bushel in Chicago—Steamer N. P. Hawks—Murder of John Campbell—Lynching of the Driscoll's—No Place for Boys—Watching the Stable for Horse Thieves—The Devil of the *Rockford Star*—Communications in the *Rockford Star*.

The winter of 1842-3 was the most remarkable in the severity and long continuance of cold, as well as the great amount of snowfall, that has ever transpired since the first settlement of the county. Among my memorandum of "Early Days," I find a record in letters and figures as follows: "The river froze over November 19, 1842" which I assume to be correct, although my impressions are it was earlier. The river closed in one night during a furious snow storm, the ferry boat running freely previous to that. The earth was not frozen at the time, and remained in that condition in the thickets and beside the fences where the snow banked up to the top rails, until the first of April, 1843; on that day in the woods between Rockford and Belvidere it was two feet deep on a level. The cold was intense. I have no record of the temperature, but I do know the whisky in the jugs the teamsters carried in their sleighs, was slushy with ice, and a barrel of Judge Blackstone's whisky with a leaky faucet, that Dan Howell had on tap in his store room in the Rockford House, was connected to the floor with a pillar of ice. On the prairie where there was a fence on both sides of the road, it filled full. On the open prairie, the snow in the road was from four to six feet deep. As each passing team broke the crust, the wind filled up the track, elevating it above the surrounding surface so as to make it almost impossible for teams to pass without turning over. There was a January thaw of sufficient duration to carry off nearly all the snow on the prairie, with the exception of that in the roads and lying along the fences, when it again froze, and a fall of snow came equal to the first storm. I never heard the faintest whisper of suffering among the settlers. There was an abundance of food; too much in fact for the consumption of the people, and quite a portion of the surplus could not be sold for cash, even at a nominal price. Dressed pork from the Rock River valley, sold in the lead mines at from seventy-five to one dollar twenty-five cents per one hundred pounds, and in Chicago the highest price was less than two cents per pound. A story was current of one fellow who lost a dressed hog off his load in Pigeon Woods, and when his neighbor behind called his attention to it, drove on without halting to pick it up, saying "it don't weigh but a hundred." I was in Galena during the thaw in January, and when I left the town, the streets and surrounding hills were naked. I had left home the week before with a neighbor and a load of cheese that we peddled through Shullsburgh, New Diggings, Benton and Hazel Green. From Wadams Grove to Gratiot's Grove across the prairie it was eighteen miles without a house, the road following in most places the identical spot now occupied by the track of the Illinois Central railroad. The deer yarded in the timber, and the skin hunters drove the poor creatures with curdogs into the crust, and killed them with clubs for the hides.

To the youngsters of that winter it was a season of supreme enjoyment. To myself personally, it was glorious. While I write, memory carries me back, and I see a young fellow roaming over the snow, and stretching away through the trackless waste came visions of Paradise. Since then I've often been sleighing with a swell-box cutter, luxurious robes and silver bells, but there has never been music so sweet as that from the BELLE OF THE JUMPER.

The public balls of that day and time were as innocent and void of immorality as any of the select gatherings of modern days. We all had friends and acquaintances in Beloit, Belvidere, Newburg, and Freeport, and often visited those towns. Distance was not considered if the party wanted to go. The girls had one dress carefully treasured for special occasions, and the boys one suit, looked after with solicitude. There was always a girl with needle and skilled hands to darn or patch it as might be required. The singing and spelling schools, and particularly the candy pulls, quiltings, and fandangos in the log cabins, have never since been equaled in genuine, unalloyed fun and happiness. "Go it while you're young, when you get old you can't."

I have a letter dated at Waukesha, Wis., December 14, 1886, from Daniel Howell, in which he confirms my recollections of the low prices for produce in the early forties. Mr. Howell writes: "I am more than glad to receive your letter, and wish I could remember more to put in this. If I had some one to talk with about old times, I would remember more. I went to Rockford in May, 1840, succeeding a Mr. Johnson in the Rockford House. Haight and Oliver owned the premises. The rent was $350 per year. Board three dollars per week. Price for man and team overnight, without grain, was seventy-five cents, whisky thrown in. We could stand all that, as the whisky was a shilling per gallon. Wheat taken to Chicago sold there for three shillings per bushel ; pork seventy-five cents per hundred pounds."

In the country taverns east of Rockford the rate for man and team without grain overnight, was five shillings, with whisky upon the same terms Mr. Howell mentions. In September, 1842, I took a load of wheat to Chicago that sold for forty-two cents per bushel. There was such a jam of teams on South Water street I could not get to the warehouse without falling into line early in the day, so I carried a sample to the steam grist mill on the west side. There being no oats in the grain, it was inspected by the buyer as "red winter;" the additional price obtained about squared my bill at the "Illinois Exchange" on Lake street, Mark Beaubien proprietor, who kept that hostlery, fiddle included, after the manner and style recorded in the early pages of these "REMINISCENES."

Early in 1841, a small steamboat, the "N. P. Hawks," built by a man of that name at some place near the headquarters of the Rock, came down the river and lay at the landing on the east bank for some weeks while a cabin was being constructed on the deck of the boat. The vessel had grounded repeatedly while on the trip, but finally reached the Mississippi some time during the summer and remained there, to the great disappointment of the people, and particularly so to those who had assisted, or promised to assist in its construction, with the expectation that the boat would make regular trips on the Rock during the season of navigation. This boat left Rockford about the 22nd of June 1841, as Mr. Howell writes me that with Mr. Haight he accompanied the vessel to Dixon, and while on their way back, at Oregon City, they heard of the murder by the Driscolls, of John Campbell, President of the Ogle county Regulators, and joining the party of citizens from that town made their way to Washington Grove, where the Rockford posse had William Driscoll in custody.

The lynching of the Driscolls was one of the few stirring events of that time in this neighborhood at which I was not present. When I went home for my horse, my father forbid my going, saying it was "no place for boys," and he kept such supervision of my riding nag, that I had no opportunity to get astride of him. Only those who have passed through a like ordeal can understand the intense excitement that pervaded the community. The loss of his team was often utter ruin to the settler, and he was ready to protect his property regardless of preliminary legal proceedings. My father who was a light sleeper, has come to my bed in a dark night telling me to get up and go to the stable. My gun was heavily charged for such occasions and I would slip out of the house and crawl on my hands and knees about the yard. On one occasion (this was at Harlem) the dogs just at night, drove a man out from under the bridge across Willow Creek. For the next three consecutive nights I lay in the manger in the stable with my gun beside me, and would have been justified in shooting any man who opened the door at unseemly hours. Fortunately or unfortunately, as the case may be, I was not subjected to the trial.

For the six months preceding the lynching, I was the "devil" in the office of the "*Rockford Star*." Philander Knappen editor, and had developed unusual speed and accuracy as a compositor, but was almost useless in all other branches of the craft, the result being that I was kept at the case, the manuscript in particular being my copy. The schooling I received in the printing office was all I ever had after I came to Rockford, and has been invaluable to me in after years. As this may be a fitting occasion to relate my further connection with the "art preservative," I will add that after the dissolution of the "*Star*," I assisted in the distribution of the "pi," and getting out the first four numbers of the "*Pilot*" which succeeded it. Early in the winter of 1841-2 I entered the office of the "*Chicago Democrat*," where I remained some two months or more, and might have become a full-fledged printer, but for the attempt of "Long John" to have me carry stove wood from the printing office on the third floor of No. 107 Lake street, to his private office adjoining the City Hotel on Clarke street. I bolted at this, telling Mr. Wentworth he might remove his office to Sheol for all I cared, and abandoned the craft then and there for all time.

The material in the "*Star*" office was owned by D. S. Haight, Daniel Howell, Adam Keith, and possibly some others; Knappen being simply a tenant. He had been in Rockford but a short time, and did not realize the temper and determination of the settlers to rid themselves from thieves, of whom the Driscolls and Broadies were the most prominent. At the time of the destruction of the office, Knappen was living at Harlem with a newly married wife. Word was sent to him of what had been done, and he speedily put in an appearance. The raiders had simply taken the forms of one side of the paper and turned them upside down on the floor, and they were not in very bad shape either. When Knappen came he stirred the "pi" laying on the floor with the stove shovel, and mixed the fonts of type in every case in the office. He turned over the subscription list to Howell of the Rockford House, where the office force boarded, and abandoned the whole thing. I do not think "Dan." realized a dollar from the assets placed in his hands. In his editorial opposing the measures of the regulators, Knappen hoped to increase the circulation of his paper, and to bring notoriety upon himself. He gave both sides a hearing in the "*Star*," as will appear in the two following communications which I have been requested to publish. I put them in type myself, and they went the rounds of the Union. The one signed "Vox

Populi," I presume to have been written by Jacob B. Miller. The one signed "B." I know to have been written by Charles Latimer. He also edited the "Pilot," (although his name did not appear in the paper,) until the advent of John A. Brown.

From the Rockford Star of July 1, 1841.

ARSON AND MURDERS.
A HEART-RENDING SCENE.

To the Editor of the Rockford Star:

Would to God that the veil of oblivion might be drawn over the scenes of bloodshed which have been lately enacted in our neighborhood; but they are too glaring to escape the world's gaze, and too revolting to civilization and the laws of humanity not to receive the just reprobation of every law and order-loving individual. To prevent misrepresentations and exaggeration, it may be well to give an authentic account of the proceedings up to this time, of the "Ogle County Lynching Club"—a Banditti organized a few weeks since in the adjoining county south of us, composed of persons who appreciate the truth of the saying that "in union there is strength," for the purpose of visiting with summary punishment any individual or individuals who might cross them, or in any manner offend a member of the "club." Banditti-like, after organization, these fiends in human shape scoured the surrounding country for plunder—not, perhaps, valuable goods, but the liberties and *lives* of their fellow citizens! Everyone who happened to fall under the suspicion of one or more of their gang was at once brought before their self-constituted tribunal, where there was no difficulty in procuring the ready testimony for convicting him of any crime which should be named, when he was sentenced, and men appointed to inflict the adjudged punishment; which in the embryo existence of "clan," generally consisted in giving the culprit from 20 to 300 lashes, well laid on the bare back, and ordering him, under the penalty of receiving "a double dose next time," to leave the country immediately. Things went on gloriously for the "gang" some considerable time. A great number of convictions took place; and the sentences were executed without opposition from the victims. At length they "caught a Tartar;" some poor fellow who had been forced to feel the iron grasp of the mob from such testimony as had been manufactured for finding him guilty, set himself at work for revenge, actuated by the same spirit manifested by the "Lynchers." A sawmill belonging to John Long, one of the Bandits, was about this time burned—the work undoubtedly of some innocently whipped individual. Long resigned and retired from the club. A new scene of lynching was now commenced, in which every one the least liable to suspicion of setting fire to the mill or any other offense, was made to feel the lash. Soon after these outrages, as might have been looked for by every one acquainted with human nature, Campbell—the then captain—was shot by two of the subjects of the displeasure of the mobocrats. It was done in the light of day, at his own house, in the presence of several witnesses, in a manner that bespoke the spirit of revenge for injuries innate in the breast of every human being, reckless of consequences. David Driscoll and William Bridge were proven to be the perpetrators of the crime. This occurred last Sunday, 26th of June.

Now, as a matter of course, the excitement was alarming. The people of this vicinity, as well as from the neighboring towns of Daysville, Oregon City and Rockford, turned out on Monday for the avowed purpose of arresting, if possible, the persons who had thus outraged the laws of the land. They met upon the scene of the unfortunate occurrence, and, without making the first effort to pursue and bring to justice the guilty, forthwith took into custody John Driscoll (the father of David Driscoll, who assisted in the murder of Campbell,) and his son William, and after burning to the ground their dwellings and outbuildings, lodged them for the time being in Oregon jail.

On Tuesday they were escorted by the mob to Washington Grove, in Ogle county, four miles from Oregon, when and where the usual one-sided exparte trial in cases of suspicion, was granted them. After raking and scraping testimony from every nook and corner of the promiscuous assemblage, some of whom were in attendance merely "to see the fun," even that jury could find them guily of nothing more henious than a blood connection to David, one of the individuals for whose blood they thirsted !—thus reasoning that they were accessory to depriving Campbell of his life. They were therefore sentenced to be executed, and one hour only was granted them to prepare for that "journey from whence no traveler returns." The friends of the victims of mobocracy will, perhaps, be pleased to learn that two clerical gentlemen with the "klan" kindly volunteered their official services in this case of emergency, and prayed with them that "the Lord would have mercy on their souls." The hour having expired, they were blindfolded and led forth to the distance of some ten steps from the demons who were now ravenous for their blood, and fired upon by each of the bandits who had a heart to do murder when he feared not the strong arm of the law, on account of the great number engaged in the horrid scene.

To the praise of humanity be it recorded that many of the mobocrats, upon "sober second thought," were anxious to retrace their steps—undo what they had done, by reprieving the prisoners. But their efforts to do away in their thinking moments what they had done in the heat of excitement, without reflection as to the legality or consequences of the same, were of no avail—they were the weaker party; and the Driscoll's were literally cut in fragments by charges from rifles, muskets, and shot guns, while many who voted for the measure, upon witnessing it, became sick at heart and fainted. Some there were in that gang who had determined to imbrue their hands in the blood of the Driscoll's, and upon their heads be the crime. They are equally as guilty of murder as David Driscoll and William Bridge; and imagination will depict the ghosts of the murdered men hovering near them night and day, while they live.

No one pretends that John and William Driscoll had committed murder; nor can they say that they merited the punishment they received, even had they been found guilty by an impartial jury of their country, of the crime alleged by the mob. No; had unimpeachable testimony been brought to bear to prove them guilty of that which circumstantial evidence was horribly distorted to convict them, the penalty would have been but three to five years imprisonment in the penitentiary.

To show the character of some who were engaged in this horrible tragedy, I will state that some three weeks since, John Driscoll was arrested for some alleged misdemeanor, by the "Lynching Club," and, after being threatened with whipping and death unless he revealed the names of horse-thieves and counterfeiters belonging to the tribe, consented to give the names of certain persons suspected by him, intimating at the same time that some of the members of the "club"—then present—would curse the day that the disclosures had been extorted. An almost unanimous cry was raised, and he was set at liberty.

And has it come to this—that in a land of civilization and Christianity, blessed with a wholesome code of laws as man's ingenuity ever invented, a few desperadoes shall rise up and inflict all manner of punishment—even DEATH—upon whomsoever they please! Shall all civil law be sacrificed and trampled in the dust at the shrine of mobocracy? Shall the life and property of no one receive any protection from the civil law, but both be subject to the nod of an inconsiderate and uncontrollable mob? Shall these things be so; or will the people rise up en masse and assert the supremacy of the laws of the land, and enforce the same against the marauders and lynchers? The latter course is certainly pointed out by JUSTICE; and I trust in God that justice will yet be meted out to all who have had a hand in this bloody business.   VOX POPULI.

Kishwaukee, June 30, 1841.

MURDER.

SUMMARY EXECUTION OF THE MURDERERS.

An excitement growing out of an attempt to suppress and rid the neighborhood of a gang of horse thieves and counterfeiters, that have for a long time infested this and the adjoining counties of DeKalb and Ogle, has resulted in the murder on Sunday last, of John Campbell, and subsequent summary execution of two of the gang of thieves and murderers.

To the people of this vicinity it is hardly necessary to state that nearly ever since the first settlement of this region of the state, it has been overrun by a host of horse thieves and counterfeiters, which no means within the power of the law or its officers could restrain. Unprovided with jails as this newly settled country is, they have been apprehended only to escape and renew their depredations; emboldened by their numbers, and the absence of civil power, they had begun to inflict punishment on those who dared to be active in their efforts to bring them to punishment. About three weeks ago a society was formed in the county most infested by these depredators, to detect and bring them to punishment. The first act of the gang was immediately to burn the saw mill of Mr. John Long, who was chosen chief of the society. A threatening letter was written about the same time by Wm. Driscoll, one of the gang, defying the society to combat, and threatening the members with personal violence, and an effort was made to concentrate the gang at his house, and to fortify and defend themselves. But it appears that alarmed at the danger of being outnumbered and lynched, they separated without waiting the arrival of the people who turned out to capture them. However, the people succeeded in capturing two or three brothers named Barrett, who had in their possession at the time, one or two stolen horses. They were committed to the jail of Ogle county, from which in a few days they escaped. The company also flogged two fellows named Daggert and Bowman, and notified the family of Driscoll's to leave the country in 15 or 20 days. This they were not disposed quietly to do, and Wm. Driscoll publicly expressed his opinion that it would be proper to shoot the chief of the society as had been done in Iowa, and that would scatter the company. Mr. Long's mill being burnt, and apprehending greater injury, he resigned his position in the society and Mr. Campbell was selected in his place. The latter was a gentleman of great respectability, a member of the Baptist church in this place, and on Sunday last was at church here.

That evening just at dusk as he was passing from his house to his stable, he was accosted by two persons. He had only time to utter

"Driscoll," and to attempt to leap behind a gate post when one of them shot him through the heart. His wife, who witnessed the deed, ran toward her fallen husband and cried, "Driscoll, you have shot my husband!"

Mr. Campbell's son, about 13 years of age, seized his father's gun, approached the murderers within a few steps, and snapped it three times at one of them. They walked off deliberately. These persons were David Driscoll and a notorious thief named Bridge. Of course the terror and excitement of the neighborhood was intense and terrible. No honest man's life or property was safe in the neighborhood. The whole country was next morning in arms—a few of our own townsmen went to the scene on Monday. The father, John Driscoll, and two of his sons were apprehended. David and Bridge had made their escape. The prisoners were taken that night to the jail at Oregon. The next morning they were taken to Washington Grove, four or five miles from Oregon. Some two hundred and fifty people were assembled there to sit in judgment upon them. One of the sons was discharged there being no proof against him. But the father, John Driscoll, and his oldest son William, were found guilty of counseling and aiding in the murder, and upon the motion of the son-in-law of the murdered John Campbell, it was resolved, unanimously, that they should be shot. One hour was given them to prepare for death, during a part of which time they joined a clergyman in prayer. At the expiration of the hour, the father was brought forth and shot, and as soon as possible thereafter the son suffered the same fate. They were both buried on the spot where they were executed.

It is proper to observe here, that however abhorrent these facts may appear to those who neither know nor can appreciate the terrible state of dismay into which the people have been thrown and kept by the desperate deeds of these people, many of the most respectable citizens were most active in the proceedings.

It is a terrible state of society, but when law is too weak to protect, there is no security but in the resort to such means as heaven has given us for self-preservation.

Mr. Campbell left a wife and six children, some of them quite young. Both Driscoll's had families.

Of the particular facts proven against the Driscoll's upon their trial, I have not been informed, but after the trial Wm. Driscoll confessed that he had been concerned in the murder of five different persons, and in the robbery of a great many stores, and that he knew of the intended murder of John Campbell. B.

Rockford, July 1, 1841.

CHAPTER VIII.

Barking Up Hill— The Only Boy in 1837.—Parties Who Pied the *Star* Office—A Grand Scoop—First Barber—Playing Brag with a Nigger—Beauty of Rock River - Swimming with a Horse—Strawberries in 1837—Mrs. Giles C. Hard's Description of the Ford—First Bridge—Jesse Blinn on Bridges—Bridge Committee—Derastus Harper Designs the Bridge—Description of the Bridge—Gone to the Hades—The First Man to Ride Across the Bridge—High Water in 1844—The First Dam—Pioneer Manufacturers—St. James Roman Catholic Church—First Watch Maker—First Bakers—First Lumber Dealers—First Lumber Dealers on the East Side—Black Walnut Lumber—First Orchard—First Nursery in Ogle County—Death of Col. Whitney the Pioneer Nurseryman.

Possibly it may have occurred to some of the readers of these "REMINISCENCES," why it is that I, a boy in his first teens, should write so confidently and from personal knowledge, of scenes and events in and about the town in which grown men only were the actors? The explanation is this. I was city bred, born, and brought up in a large hotel, and from infancy had been trained not to take apparent notice of, and more especially never to speak about, or to comment upon the acts or conversations among the guests of the house. So confident was my father of the result of his training, that upon one occasion, when told I knew all about an affair it was desired to keep shady, the old gentleman replied, "Well, if they expect to get it out of John Henry they're barking up hill."

In 1837, I was the only boy in town of thirteen years or more, and this Masonic trait becoming known, I was freely admitted into all the councils, games, and pastimes of the town, and this continued during the lifetime of most of the actors. When the *Star* office was "pied," by a mere accident I knew who did it, and the parties were aware of my knowledge; they also knew I would not betray them. I never breathed a syllable of this for thirty years after, when I told an editor of one of the local papers, that D. S. Haight, Charles Latimer, and Adam Keith were the men. To make a grand scoop for his paper, he came out that week giving details of the affair, and also of other similar items I related to him pertaining to still earlier days, stating them in such language as to leave the impression he wrote from personal knowledge. He was six miles away at the time; had no acquaintance with some of the parties, and knew nothing except from hearsay.

Reuben W. Armstrong, an "American citizen of African descent," who came here from Columbia, Lancaster county, Penn., was the first barber in the town. He opened his shop in the summer of 1845, in the basement of the "Arcade," Potter & Preston's brick building on the southwest corner of State and Madison streets. Previous to his advent, the boys cut hair for each other. In some instances a fellow with his hat off presented a most grotesque appearance. In the summer of 1837, George Miller, whose hair was black and curled, got out of the chair with a cross an inch wide on the back of his head where the hair had been shaved bare to the skin. "Rube" was a sport of superior skill; a trait of character which may be inherit in the family, and competed successfully with any of Caucasian blood whom he could induce to play with him. I recall an incident in the early fifties, when a party of players in Peake's block were about to be raided by the police, when a prominent white man went out through the window taking the sash with him, rather than be found playing brag with a nigger.

The beauty of Rock River has frequently been extolled in recent years by travelers and residents of the valley, whose appreciation of the lovely landscapes shown from its head waters to the Mississippi, have found expression in both prose and verse. The present condition of the stream, disfigured as it is by the hand of man, can give but a faint conception of the appearance of its banks in a state of nature.

In the immediate vicinity of Rockford, the remarkable beauty of the landscape excited my admiration, city bred boy as I was, when I followed the trail along the bank gun in hand, intent on potting a stray duck, while keeping a sharp lookout for the wild onions and the fish on my set lines, with which to eke out our scanty larder. The banks were bold and sodded to the edge of the water. There were no gullies where the sod had been cut out by running water; little or none of the timber had been cut, and the earth was literally covered with flowers. In places, the bottom of the stream was nearly covered with clams and piles of shells a foot or more in depth, which the muskrats left close to the edge of the water were frequent. We tried to prepare these clams for our table. I gathered half a bushel in twenty minutes in the immediate vicinity of the ferry landing in the summer of 1837, only to find they were too tough for my sound teeth; and too, they seemed to destroy the flavor of the Hoosier bacon with its accompaniment of live stock, to which I had become accustomed.

Opposite to what is now Knightville, were two islands, the upper and larger one having a few small trees growing on its surface; the lower one covered with grass only. Some ten rods above Jonathan Peacock's place, was an island of about two acres, on which were oak trees twenty inches in diameter and a dense thicket of wild fruit. Just below this island was a sand bar ten to fifteen rods long. The main channel of the stream was on the east shore, and it was here we went in swimming. I wonder if the youngsters of the present day know how to manage horses in deep water, a knowledge essential to a pioneer? My pony was as tractable in deep water as a dog, and we both learned the art there under the instructions of a Hoosier. If you must swim for life or necessity, strip the horse of all trappings except the briddle; unbuckle the throatlatch in order to get rid of it if required; separate the reins, which should not exceed three and one-half feet in length, and when the animal is in deep water grasp the hair of the mane close to the withers with the hand holding the reins and lie down on his back. He may be guided by the reins or by patting his neck on either side with the disengaged hand; more especially so if he is a trained riding nag.

Just above the present site of the water works the channel shifted abruptly to the west shore. There was a dense thicket on the site of Thomas Scott's coal yard and the Kenosha car tracks. Below State street, and extending to the ford was a grove of tall, thrifty white oak timber. The bluff below the ford was sodded to the edge of the water and crowned with a row of red cedar trees. In June, 1837, for a week or two, the side of this bluff was fairly red with strawberries. On the west shore below the abutments of the C. & N. W. railway bridge, the river widened abruptly, and the banks were lined with tall timber to the mouth of the creek. Above this bridge for half a mile the ground as far west as Main street, was covered with brush eight to ten feet high, with an occasional black oak tree. In June there were acres here where one could not step without crushing the strawberries. Some twenty rods above G. A. Sanford's residence on Main street, and extending west in places as far as Court street, was a thicket of twenty acres or more, so dense as to be impassable except at the expense of torn clothing and loss of time. At the ferry landing on the east side, the bank rose by a succession of steps, the first of about six feet, the next of fifteen, when it was level for some ten or twelve rods; the wagon trail at this point meeting the foot of the hill 150 feet north of State street, when it turned southeast, reaching the top of the hill at the intersection of State and Madison streets, where the earth has been cut down nearly or quite fifteen feet.

The ford was the only one on the river below the mouth of the Peeketolika (that was the way it was spelled in the report of the first election in 1836) which could be relied upon in ordinary stages of water. For not less than 150 feet in width, the depth of water, which in summer just covered the forward axle of a wagon, did not vary six inches, the rock bottom being as smooth as a floor.

Mrs. Giles C. Hard, whose husband was the ferryman in 1841-2 and earlier, speaks of this ford as "a most useful highway just as nature formed it, I saw worlds of covered wagons, cattle, horses, hogs and sheep trailing across the ford, the most of them going to settle in Stephenson county. No ferry such as we had, could have taken across the river all the people and stock that I saw ford the stream during the low water of 1841-2."

In the forties, a law was smuggled through the legislature taxing the river counties for the improvement of the navigation of the stream. A coffer dam some fifty feet wide was built through the rapids, a wheel at the lower end propelled by the current bailed the water out, and a steamboat channel excavated in the fall and winter of 1845-6, the rock being piled just outside the dam. It ruined the ford and was absolutely useless for navigation, as the rapids at the mouth of the river in ordinary stages of water, would not float a steamer.

The first bridge at State street was not the first bridge across the river in the county. In the winter of 1844-5, I crossed the river with a horse and buggy on a bridge at Roscoe, and I crossed on foot at Rockton (Pecatonica then) on the stringers of a bridge at that place.

In my scrap book I find an item relating to early bridges, in the remarks made by Jesse Blinn at the re-union held at the Holland House, Thursday, February 9, 1871, by the "Rockford Society of Early Settlers." To the fourth toast—"The descendants of the Pioneers of Winnebago County, chips of the old block," Mr. Blinn made a few pertinent remarks. He "did not believe, and it was no discredit perhaps to the chips, that they could not fill the places and endure the hardships of the "old blocks." That with all our boasted generosity, a liberality that bestows princely sums for almost every conceivable object, yet it falls short today of that of the old blocks! What did they do? We had no court house or jail; there were no bridges across the river, the old, slow, poking ferry must be used or the people could not cross the river. The land had come in market before the settlers had obtained money sufficient to pay for it, and many of them had to borrow money at exorbitant rates of interest. This had not been repaid; and they were struggling on, poor crops and low prices came year after year, yet they wanted bridges, a court house and a jail, and the old blocks said let us build; and they did build. Many of you remember that in one season we built the present court house and jail, fenced them in and *gave them* to the county, and also five bridges across Rock river. One here, one at Roscoe, one where the iron bridge now stands at Rockton, one at 'Macktown,' and one above the mouth of the Pecatonica."

I also find in my scrap book an item stating that the building committee for the first bridge at State street were "E. H. Potter, Daniel Howell, Williard Wheeler, C. I. Horsman, and G. A. Sanford." It was built by subscription, and my impression is the largest cash donation, came from Frink & Walker, the stage proprietors.

Derastus Harper, who resided on the west side, designed and erected the bridge. He possessed mechanical skill and ingenuity of a high order. He afterwards went to Chicago, where he became the city engineer. He designed and built the first pivot bridge across the Chicago river. I make this statement about the pivot bridge from a conversation I recall to memory between the late John Beattie, Wm. F. Ward, (who were house joiners of acknowledged skill,) and myself.

The State street bridge was of three strings of lattice work made from oak planks fastened together with oaken pins. It was as tough as whalebone, and although it wabbled and shook from end to end when loaded with one or more of the six horse teams that crossed the stream, it never went down when there was a support between the shore end of the lattice and the water. None of the structures which succeeded it, could have sustained a tythe of the grief this old bridge endured.

Mr. Harper laid out and framed the bridge on the ground, commencing at the shore on west State street, extending in the direction of the present site of the Silver Plate works. Each plank of the lattice was laid in position and the holes bored by hand, when one or more pins were inserted to hold them in position. There was no iron used save the nails that held the half inch basswood boards which covered the lattice when the structure was finally completed. There were abutments of stone on each shore. On Christmas night, 1844, the lattice was in place for about seventy feet from the west shore, supported by temporary trestles; ice had formed about the trestles from the west side; the water rose lifting the whole structure, trestles included, when it tipped over with a tremendous crash. There was a ball that night at the Rockford House, and when the sound came, we of the male persuasion bolted for the river, exclaiming "the bridge has gone to the hades." We did not then realize the skill and ingenuity of Mr. Harper as a bridge builder, or the admirable qualities of the material he had selected, which the limited means of the people could supply. The fallen lattice was hauled out of the water, each plank numbered with red chalk, and aside from a few that were splintered, they were again placed in proper order. The bridge was opened for travel July 4th, 1845, and it was estimated 2,000 people crossed that day. When the last plank was laid, E. H. Potter mounted a horse standing there, and was the first man to ride across the bridge, so he afterwards told William A. Manning, now residing at Santa Barbara, California.

There were two roadways, separated by the center lattice which projected about five feet above the planking; the rule of the road being the same then as now, passengers kept to the right, those of the male persuasion vaulting over the lattice when the inclination prompted.

The dam, which was above the bridge near the present site of the water works, broke three times after the bridge was completed. The first time near the west end in the spring of 1846. The next time in the spring of 1847, taking the saw mill of Phelps, Daniels & Gregory on the east side, disarranging the trestles of the bridge on each occasion, and getting the lattice out of line.

June 1st, 1851, the old dam went out breaking away at the west bulk head. The rush of water carried away an acre or more on the west bank and also undermined and swung to the east, the lower ends of the first two trestles from the west bank, and disarranging some of the others, letting the south lattice down about seven feet below the other side. Either side was still available for foot passengers, and a horse could have been led or rode across with safety on the upper side had necessity required, but the ford was preferred. With a tythe of the present machinery available, the bridge could have been raised and made passable in a few days, but the only material at hand was a scant supply of rope and blocks; and too, there was no one competent to direct the work who would take it in hand. After several abortive attempts, William F. Ward was persuaded to oversee the work. Under his direction it was finally raised and put to use. It was as crooked as a cow path, and shook and wabbled from center to circumference, but held on faithfully to the last, when it was re-placed in 1854 by the covered bridge.

The high water in 1844 throughout the northwest does not appear to have been mentioned in late years. What the flood may have been on the lower Mississippi I do not know, but at and below St. Louis the river was twenty miles wide, flooding the American Bottom from three to twenty feet deep. At St. Louis, steamboats were loaded from the windows of the second story of the stores on the levee. At Kaskaskie, in this state, a steamboat ran out two miles from the main stream, laid the gang plank from the deck into the window of a nunnery there and took the women aboard. A young fellow who was trying to open a farm on the American Bottom opposite St. Louis, caught a hog-trough floating down stream, and paddled across the river in it to the west shore. I saw in Galena, in 1845, a steamboat that had grounded 300 miles up the river, on the prairie three miles from the channel; the water fell and left her high and dry. The machinery was taken out and preparations made to burn the hull for the purpose of securing the iron, when the water rose and floated the boat into the channel. In this vicinity the roads for most of the summer were nearly impassable for anything but oxen. Merchandise was hauled from Chicago with a team of three or four yokes of oxen, the driver riding through the creeks and sloughs on the yoke between the heads of the wheelers, controlling the team with a Hoosier whip, which with the lash, measured thirty feet or more in length. There has been no such season of continued high water in this locality since that year.

From my scrap book, from personal recollections, and from items supplied to me by Messrs. James B. Howell, L. B. Gregory, and from Mr. John Nettleton, now of Los Angeles, California, I have compiled the following account of the old dam.

The dam was located a few rods above the present site of the water works. Just above this place the main channel of the stream shifted abruptly from the east to the west shore. On the east side at the location of the dam, the water for two-thirds the width of the stream, was about waist deep in summer, with eight to nine feet in the channel. To the best of my recollection, the reason this site was selected was the general belief that if the dam was located at the head of the rapids, the town, as well as the business centre, would concentrate there. And too, another reason may have existed. Had it been built at the ford on the rock bottom the material would have cost cash, a commodity the promoters of the enterprise did not possess except to a limited extent, while timber, brush, stone and earth could be made available at the site chosen.

The mill race on the east side extended to Walnut street, and was about twenty feet wide. At this point Williard Wheeler had a saw mill. Just above, James B. Howell had carding and fulling machinery. At State street, on the south side of the street, was Nettleton's grist mill. At the head of the race, A. C. Spafford and L. B. Gregory had a saw mill. There may have been other machinery in operation when the dam broke, but the above is all that I recall on the east side. On the west side at the head of the race was a saw mill built by Thomas D. Robertson and Charles I. Horsman. Just below this mill Oriando Clark had an iron foundry in a stone building. The race on the west side was about fifteen rods long.

A Mr. Edward S. Hanchett, who resided in Freeport, had charge of the construction of the dam when it was first commenced, the promoters of the enterprise supplying the material on the banks. Mr. Hanchett had built one or more dams on the Pecatonica in the vicinity of Freeport previous to his advent here. He finally abandoned the work and C. C. Coburn, who resided here for many years after, completed the job.

Mr. L. B. Gregory supplies me with the following: "John Phelps, J. T. Daniels, and L. B. Gregory built the saw mill on the east side, and I think started in the fall or winter of 1845. T. D. Robertson and C. I. Horsman built the saw mill on the west side. I do not know when it started or that it ever did much sawing. The dam broke three times; first near the west end, I think in the spring of 1846; the next I think was in the spring of 1847 near the east end and took off our saw mill, landing two bents down on Long's island. A. C. Spafford bought Daniels out and I bought out Phelps. Spafford and I brought the timbers back and got the mill sawing in the spring of 1848. The last break was June 1st, 1851."

From Mr. James B. Howell I have the following: "The enterprise in which I was interested consisted of wool carding and cloth dressing. The first situation on lot 5, block D. The foundation walls were built in 1845 and the structure in 1846. Owing to the repeated breaking away of the dam, water for power was not supplied until July, 1848, when work was commenced, and long waiting ceased. The one machine for carding when complete, cost me nearly or quite $500, and the cloth dressing apparatus fully as much more, while the whole outfit including lot, building, and power to propel the works, reached a totel of $2,000 or more."

"When the old dam gave away, which it did on the first day of June, 1851, I removed the carding machine to New Milford, and ran it in an upper room of Mr. Fountain's factory, returning to Rockford in June, 1852, and as soon as water was let into the race, was ready for operations again. I have the pleasure of believing that my wheels, both under the old and present power, were the first to do service in Rockford."

Mr. John Nettleton, now of Los Angeles, California, writes me in relation to the first grist mill in Rodkford, which was built by his father and himself.

"Moses Nettleton, my father, was born near the village of Prescott, Augusta township, Canada, in 1798, from which place he emigrated in 1839 and settled in Ogle county, Illinois. In the fall of 1844, he in company with myself, went to Rockford, and after investigating the water power he contracted for the lot on the east side of the river next south of the city bridge, and also for water to run a mill. The following winter—1844-5, we got out timber for the frame, and saw logs for lumber, near Jefferson, Wisconsin, to inclose the mill, which we floated down the river in the spring of 1845. Before reaching Beloit, we learned that both the Beloit and Rockford dams had gone out in the high water, and we tied up our rafts and went down the stream to investage. During the following summer we floated the timber to Rockford, got stone and laid the foundation for the mill. I think the mill was started sometime in the year 1846, but am not certain as I was absent. L. B. Gregory and A. C. Spafford can give you more accurate information as to the time of starting the mill than I can. It was first started with two run of stone, to which a third was added about two years afterwards. It cost between three and four thousand dollars."

I have been able to obtain but little official data from which to give the early history of St. James Roman Catholic Church, the first of that denomination in the county. The Rev. Father Flaherty, who now has charge of the parish, examined all the documents in his possession and supplied me with such information as they contained. I also wrote to Bishop Feehan, asking the date of dedication, etc., and received a reply from the Chancellor, which is here appended. This, together with my personal recollections, is all the information I could secure.

"CHANCERY OFFICE, Chicago, Dec. 16, 1890.

DEAR SIR:—In regard to St. James, Rockford, I am sorry that I find very little information, as nearly all our records were destroyed in the 'Big Fire.' The oldest deed I find is of 1851, conveying from Artemas Hitchcock and Mary his wife, to Rt. Rev. James Oliver Van de Viller, for the sum of $150, lot No. 1, in block 26, as found in the map of the village drawn by Duncan Ferguson. Second, a conveyance (warranty deed,) from John Lee and wife Catherine, to Anthony Regan, Bishop of Chicago, for $400, lot No. 2, in block 26. The first is recorded February 15, 1851. The second, August 17, 1855. This is all I can ascertain concerning the early days of Rockford.

Very truly, P. J. MULDOON, Chancellor."

From Father Flaherty's notes gathered from the books of the church, "the first record of baptism is by John A. Hampston. He was in charge from 1851 until 1854." Father Hampston, who died while in charge of the parish and was buried under the church building, I remember quite well. He was of studious habits, modest and retiring in manner, and highly respected by the few outside his congregation who made his acquaintance. The church building was a small one story wood structure, to which the citizens of the town contributed a portion of the means with which to erect it.

Alexander Brazee, from Brandon, Vermont, was the first watch repairer to locate in Rockford. I am told he first opened his shop in 1840 on the west side, on the site of Daniel Dow's block. Personally, I do not recall his presence there as so early a date, but I do know his shop was there the winter of the deep snow—1842-3. In the fall of 1841, Mr. Brazee occupied the front room of Tinker & Johnson's tailor shop on the site of No. 322 East State street, and for some years afterwards was located at 303 East State street. He built the two story and basement brick dwelling which stood on the southwest corner of First and Oak streets, known as the "pepper-box." He went across the plains to California in 1850, and about 1852-3 died in Oregon.

Wyman & Houghten (Ephriam Wyman and Bethel Houghten,) were the first bakers. They opened a boarding house and bakery in the spring of 1838, in the building now standing, No. 506 South Main street. Mr. Wyman was born in Lancaster, Mass., January 26, 1809; he arrived at Rockford, September 20, 1835. Mr. Houghton came from Keene, New Hampshire, where he was born in 1808; he came to Rockford in the fall of 1836. When Wyman arrived there were three families on the east side: Daniel S. Haight, Eliphalet Gregory, and James Wood. On the west side: Germanicus Kent, John Wood, and James Boswell.

John Edwards, a native of Acton, Mass., was the first dealer in pine lumber in the town. Mr. Edwards came to Rockford in 1850, his family arriving the following year. His first yard was near the present site of the Union Foundry and Peter Sames' wagon factory, near the Northwestern railway tracks. Most of the lumber he had while at this place came by team from St. Charles, and the amount of stock on hand at any one time from ten to twelve thousand feet. Afterwards his yard was located on the northwest corner of Church and State streets, the lumber being hauled from Elgin. He did not pile the lumber at either locality as is the rule at present, each wagon load being packed by itself. Prices as given by a member of his family were: $24 to $30 for No. 1; $18 to $20 for No. 2; $14 to $18 for No. 3. At times he had great difficulty in getting the lumber from the end of the track at Elgin, as the teamsters who had hauled wheat to that place, would throw off half the load in Pigeon Woods when stalled in the mud, and leave it there.

Regan & Perry (M. H. Regan from Canada—Seely Perry from Massachusetts) were the first to establish a yard of pine lumber on the east side of the river in 1851, on the northeast corner of State and Second streets. The lumber came from Chicago to the end of the track of the Galena & Chicago Union R. R.; the average amount of stock carried the first year, being about 50,000 feet, at a price in the vicinity of $12 per m. Since this yard was first established, Mr. Perry has been continuously engaged in the lumber trade, being now identified with the Rockford Lumber and Fuel Company.

Before the advent of the railroad, the local dealers at times had a few pine boards for sale, which had been brought out from Chicago by the teams hauling wheat to the lake port, the freight being from five to six dollars per m. and paid in "store pay."

There was quite a large quantity of black walnut timber on the

Pecatonica bottoms and elsewhere, which was cut and used freely for local consumption in the early days. The siding of Haight's dwelling house on the corner of State and Madison streets, was of black walnut, as was most of the studding and siding of the Washington House. In the fall of 1838, I gathered the nuts in the immediate vicinity of Trask's bridge, and could readily have secured a wagon box full within a quarter of a mile of the crossing place. In recent years I have heard it remarked upon, that the early settlers should have been so shiftless as to have cut this timber which has since become so valuable. It goes to show how little some of the present generation understand the conditions of life as they then existed; for a short experience only is required, to prove that the proper time to use material of this kind, is when it can be made available. In 1839, Reuben Barrett of Harlem, made two fence gates of black walnut lumber, which were in use on his farm at the time of his death in November, 1872.

In my scrap book I find an article cut from the *Chicago Times* of January 25th, 1878, containing a synopsis of a paper read by Jonathan Periam of Chicago, at the annual meeting of the Northern Illinois Horticultural Society at Franklin Grove, Illinois, and here append such items contained in the paper as pertain to this vicinity:

"In Winnebago county the first orchard was started by Doct. George Haskell, at Rockford, in the year 1839, and some of the trees yet remain. He also established a nursery in 1840 or '41 from trees obtained at Alton. In Ogle county, orcharding was begun in '36 from grafted stock by Mr. Walmsey."

(I think this pioneer nursery in Ogle county was located about one mile and one half above Byron on the west bank of the river, where the bottom land is surrounded on the west and north sides by a high bluff, as I saw a small nursery there of trees some three feet high in the winter of 1838-9. The claim was purchased by Henry G. R. Dearborn, from Boston, Mass., and I recall the fact that the nursery was a factor in the long price paid for the improvement. J. H. T.)

"About the year 1840 the first orchard was planted in Lee county, principally of seedlings. The first nursery was established by Mr. Whitney." From my scrap book I take this item in relation to the pioneer nurseyman of Lee county, cut from the *Rockford Republican:*

["DIXON, ILL., June 12, 1891.—(Special to *The Republican*.—Col. Nathan Whitney died this morning of old age. He was born January 27, 1791. He came here in 1835, and was a commissioner to organize Lee county. He held three commissions from De Witt Clinton of New York—captain, lieutenant, and colonel. He was in the engagement at Fort Erie in the year 1812. At his death he was the oldest Mason in the world, having been initiated June 20, 1817. He planted the first nursery north of the Illinois river, and was widely known all over the northwest."]

"In those old days our sauce was made of wild plums, our mince pies of crab apples and venison, soured with vinegar, sweetened with watermelon syrup or wild honey, and spiced with the pounded bark of sassafras. The prairie region of Illinois was a wilderness of grass, only pastured here and there by herds of half wild cattle, and with the log cabin and beginning of a farm at long intervals. In the year 1839, Joseph Periam built the first frame barn in Cook county. In 1838 he planted a small nursery of apple and pear seeds, peach, plum and cherry stones. In 1839 he set out the first orchard of grafted fruit in Cook county. The trees were hauled from Ohio in a wagon."

CHAPTER IX.

First County Fair in 1841 Held on the East Side—Committees—Premiums—Address by Doct. Goodhue—Locality of the Cattle Pens—Couldn't Pay Ferriage—A Pound of Sugar and a Bushel of Wheat—Couldn't Cast a Shadow—A Load of Oats for a Pair of Boots—Doct. Goodhue's Prophecy—Primitive Habits—A Sea of Grass—Where'll We Stay To-night—Pioneer of Stephenson County—His Daughters—The Cabin—Where Shall I Sleep—Disrobing—Politics in 1840—The Band—Old Jake—Arkansaw Traveler—The Harrison Ball—The Van Buren Ball—The Tickets—Doct. Crosby and the Upper Reel—Pigeon-Winging—Long John Wentworth.

I also find in my scrap book an account of the preliminary proceedings, and the first Agricultural Fair and Cattle Show held in this county, which was compiled by R. P. Porter for his History of Winnebago county, and published in the *Gazette* in 1876. This, with my personal recollections, may serve to give some idea of the agricultural situation at that time.

"The year 1841 saw the birth of the Agricultural Society. Though not the same society as the present one, it was of course the embryo from which the present association sprung. In September, a meeting was held to make the necessary arrangements for the ensuing cattle show on the 13th of October, when the following resolutions were unanimously adopted."

"*Resolved*, On motion of J. S. Norton, seconded by George W. Lee, that the Annual Fairs be held at Rockford, alternately on the east and west side of the river, commencing the present year on the east side."

"*Resolved*, That all the available funds of the Society be distributed in premiums on the day of the cattle show, and that the premiums be paid in agricultural publications."

Resolved, That George Haskell, Jonathan Weldon, and George W. Lee be a committee to prepare a code of By-Laws for the Society."

"*Resolved*, That with a view of extending the benefits of the Winnebago County Agricultural Society, of enlisting the combined efforts of the farmers of this county in sustaining the society, J. Weldon, Esq., was appointed our agent to obtain members of the society, and to collect the monies for the same, which will be devoted to the payment of the premiums at the ensuing Cattle Show."

"*Resolved*, That the Society meet at 2 o'clock p. m., on the 13th of October, and form a procession under the direction of Jason Marsh, Esq., marshal of the day, and march to the place appointed for the delivery of the address."

"*Resolved*, That Daniel S. Haight, Doct. Josiah C. Goodhue, and Charles I. Horsman be a committee of arrangements to prepare a place for a show, and make all the necessary preparations for exhibitions, rent a room for the delivery of an address, and for faciliating the passage over the ferry."

"Jason Marsh was appointed marshal of the day; Isaac N. Cunningham, J. Weldon, and Sebbens Wilson committee on horses; Milton Kilbourn, Horace Miller, and Samuel Hayes on cattle; Isaac M. Johnson, J. S. Norton, and Ezra S. Cable on sheep; Charles I. Horsman, Alonzo Corey, and Jason Marsh on cultivated lands; Benj. T. Lee, Peter Johnson, Daniel S. Haight, Peter H. Watson, and James B. Martyn, on hogs; Shepherd Leach, Henry Thurston, and William E. Dunbar on domestic articles."

"There was no necessity to print a premium list. The whole business was published in a couple of sticks of solid minion in the Rockford papers. There were seven premiums for horses, six for cattle, four for hogs, and two for sheep. One for the best cultivated ten acres of land, one for the best 25 ℔s. of butter, one for the best cheese weighing 15 ℔s., one for the best 10 yards of flannel, one for the best 50 skeins of silk manufactured in the county, and one for the best sugar made from beets in the county. This was the extent of the premiums offered in 1841 by the first cattle show ever held in Northern Illinois."

* * * * * * * * *

"The cattle pens had been erected in a little grove adjoining the village. where the various committees met at 11 a m., and forthwith proceeded to make an examination of the animals in the Society pens. The exhibition of domestic articles took place in the hall of the Rockford House. At 2 o'clock the procession formed under the direction of Jason Marsh. marshal of the day, and marched to the court house which was then on the east side, near the northwest corner of Market and First streets. Here a large crowd of ladies and gentlemen had assembled. The meeting was opened by prayer by the Rev. Mr. Joel Potter."

"It was not deemed necessary in those days to send abroad for speakers. Rockford talent was above par in 1841, so Doct. J. C. Goodhue delivered the address, of which the published report says: It was listened to very attentively. The Doctor's address was both practical and illustrative, and contained just the lessons which, if put in practice by our farmers would secure happier results to their agricultural labors. He dwelt with great effect and eloquence upon the bright prospects which await the farmers of this fertile valley, and presented a practical knowledge of the subject, which showed that he had not studied alone in the school of Esculapius. At half past five the committees handed in their reports. And thus the first Cattle Show in Northern Illinois was begun and finished in one day."

The *Rockford Pilot*, published the next day, commented on the Fair in the following terse manner:

"The cattle show came off yesterday in good style. The day was fine, the women were fine, the pigs were fine. The display of stock certainly exceeded our anticipations. Surely, we live in a wonderful age. Mobs, miracles and morality are developing in a manner that would have bothered the brains of our grandfathers. Here we are in a country that six years ago lay in the precise state in which it was moulded in the palm of the great builder—not a tenement had ever been erected in this precinct to cover the head of a white man. Yesterday we saw a thousand people collected for the great object of improvement in the science of agriculture, and a display of domestic stock that would have been creditable to any portion of the United States. We saw silk that had been manufactured by the hands of the ladies of our place, and a variety of products that show the rapid strides that we are making toward perfection in the noble science of agriculture."

Although I did not attend Doct. Goodhue's address, my recollections of the day are quite clear. The stock was exhibited in the grove on the east side, in the immediate vicinity of the northeast corner of First and Oak streets. Cattle and horses were tied to the trees, while sheep and hogs were confined in square rail pens corresponding in size to the length of a rail. Garden and other products were on exhibition in the hall of the Rockford House. Henry Thurston brought in a mammoth squash weighing 108 pounds, and took second premium; while Charles I. Horsman carried off the first premium with a specimen weighing 128 pounds. There were several loads of grain exhibited in wagons standing in the street in front of the Rockford House; among them I recall a wagon-box full of white corn on the ear—a new variety at the time—shown by John Paul, the school teacher of 1840-1, who told me he would not have been there but for the ferry being free that day, as he had no money with which to have crossed the river. At and about this time, a bushel of wheat would not buy a pound of loaf sugar, but could be exchanged for dry goods. There was no cash market for grain except to a limited extent. The tavern keepers paid ten cents per bushel for the few oats they required, and the Goodhue's of Beloit, and Judge Blackstone, whose distillery was located on Turtle Creek, six miles from that town, were occasional buyers of corn for cash, to be used in the manufacture of whisky. The Judge's expression that "the people were so d—d poor they couldn't cast a shadow," was most appropriate. Some years since, Oliver A. Larkins told me he hauled a wagon load of oats and put them in Dan. Howell's grain bin, telling Dan. that if he would pay for a pair of coarse boots for which he was indebted to E. H. Potter, it would be satisfactory.

Notwithstanding the gloomy financial outlook, Doct. Goodhue saw with prophetic eye the future destiny of this region. In the winter of 1838-9 I heard him state his firm belief that the Valley of Rock River would become the garden of the Union; that the water power at Rockford would be utilized, and the town become a second Rochester; which prophecy is nearly accomplished, as the present population of the town is almost equal to what Rochester, N. Y., possessed at that time.

The primitive habits of the people are well illustrated by an incident wherein I was one of the parties, and at a time when it may be supposed the people were comparatively well provided with the conveniences and comforts of a well ordered household.

In the fall of 1845, a young gentleman from Uniontown. Pa., well dressed, and evidently accustomed to the habits of polite society, came in the stage to Rockford, on his way to visit some friends who lived, he said, on Rock Run, twelve miles from Freeport, and he employed me to take him up there. We left Rockford in the afternoon with a horse and buggy, and I drove to Trask's bridge, crossed the Pecatonica and after driving through the timber, struck across the prairie for Rock Run. Even then the country was all open; it was literally a sea of grass, and one could drive where he pleased. When I came to a track leading in the direction I wanted to go, I took it; otherwise, straight across the prairie for a point on Rock Run twelve miles from Freeport. The young fellow was nervous with his first experience of a trip through the wilderness, and when I left a beaten track, propounded a series of questions something like this: "Where are you going?" "How do you know you are right?" "Where will we stay to-night?" "Do you see that post?" "Yes; I've noticed several of them." "What are they for?" "They are section posts. We are traveling due west on a section line that strikes Rock Run within one mile of a point twelve miles from Freeport."

Just at night we drove up to a settler's cabin and found we were two miles from our destination. In the conversation the settler ascertained where the young fellow was from, and as he had migrated from

Uniontown, he invited us to remain with him overnight. I told the young fellow we had better do so, as we might get sloughed, which he didn't exactly understand as neither of us carried any whisky, and it was decided to stay there. The settler, who was one of the pioneers of Stephenson county, had pushed out from Uniontown when a young man; had married on the frontier, and with his wife and two children—girls; one about eleven, the other perhaps fifteen years old—was then living in the original log cabin which he put up to hold the claim. It was built in true pioneer style without a nail; the roof of shakes, the door, floor and fireplace of puncheons, the fireplace lined on the inside with clay, and the chimney of split sticks laid up with mud. In one corner at that end where the fireplace was, were a few boards supported by pegs in the logs which answered as a cupboard; in the other corner at that end was a ladder to go aloft. At the opposite end of the cabin were two beds—one in each corner; one of them had a curtain suspended about it; the other had nothing of that kind, being fully exposed. After a bountiful supper, the settler produced some clay pipes, some home grown tobacco and we sat before the fire and smoked. The settler had many questions to ask of Uniontown and its people, and the young fellow was much interested in what they told him of their life, particularly so in what the wife said she had undergone in making their claim and getting it under cultivation.

The young fellow with his well-fitting clothes and pleasant easy manner, was an object of intense interest to the two girls, brought up as they were in the wilderness, and they watched his every motion, and hung upon every word he said, with ears, eyes, and mouths wide open. At the usual bed-time, I asked the wife where I should sleep? She told me there, pointing with her thumb over her shoulder at the bed without curtains. I carried my chair to the bedside, undressed as deliberately as I ever have before or since and got into the bed. Directly the young fellow asked the wife where he should sleep? She told him there, in that bed with me. He carried his chair to the side of the bed, took off his coat, vest, and necktie, laid them over the back of the chair and sat down on the bed, while all three kept up a lively conversation. The settler sat on one side of the fireplace, the two girls on the other, while the wife sat in front of and facing the fire. The young fellow pulled off his boots and finally got rid of his stockings, during all of which time they kept firing questions at him, with the two girls gazing in open-mouthed curiosity at his appearance. At last he unbuckled his suspenders, threw them over his shoulders, and sat down on the side of the bed, when it dawned on the mind of the wife that he didn't propose to pull off his trousers while the two girls were looking at him, so she spoke to her daughters and they all three went out doors, when he undressed and got into bed.

I was too young at the time to have had a personal knowledge of the inside political work going on in 1838-9, and the early forties, and can only state that being well mounted, myself and pony were frequently called upon as bearers of dispatches for the Democrats, to which party I then adhered from inheritance, and in mature years from conviction. The facilities for communication were so meagre in 1840, that the official vote of this State in the Harrison campaign, was not known until late in December. I infer the vote was intentionally kept back by the Democratic officials at Springfield. A messenger from the capital with the official vote of the State, passed through Rockford some ten days in advance of its publication in the Chicago papers, communicating the news to the prominent men of the party in each village for betting purposes, Illinois being one of the eight states that voted for Van Buren. Haight gave me the figures the same day he received them, and I carried them to my father at Harlem. Whatever may now be thought of the proceeding, the old gentleman did "bet on a sure thing;" my own share of the winnings being a pair of coarse boots.

The spareness of the population, the limited amount accessable of the current literature of the day to which some of the settlers had been accustomed; the almost entire deprivation of the pleasures of social life among the older people, caused them to enter into a political or local contest, with a vim which almost invariably became personal before it was decided. When the fight was ended, the passions cooled down, and "sober second thought" had resumed its sway, it frequent-happened that both parties joined in a general pow-wow and celebration. It was so in 1840. The Whigs of this locality imitated the tactics so successfully practiced throughout the Union. They had no cider either hard or sweet, but they did possess in abundance, all the paraphernalia used by the party in the populous parts of the country. They put up a log cabin in regular pioneer style, on the southeast corner of State and Madison streets, for political headquarters, profusely decorated with coonskins and other regalia pertaining to the times; imported speakers from Galena, Chicago, and intermediate points; got up processions, and with Frank Parker blowing an E flat bugle and China Parker a clarinet—neither of them having the slightest knowledge of music, and each blowing with might and main in a vain effort to drown out his companion—marched about the village whenever they could secure a following. The village drum was in the possession of the Democrats, and consequently not available for Whig celebrations.

Among the local Whig speakers there were none so popular as Jacob (Jake) B. Miller. Jake was a classical scholar, and when the occasion demanded, could and did present his views in most polished language of the Queen's English. He was a capital mimic, and thoroughly familiar with the vernacular of the native westerner. When addressing an assembly of this character, he used their own idiom and figures of speech made familiar in their daily life. If, as he sometimes did at the close of a harangue, he produced his fiddle and broke out with the Arkansaw Traveler, the whole assembly joined in a general breakdown and pow-wow, winding up by carrying Jake on their shoulders to the nearest bar for a smile.

The windup of this campaign resulted in two public balls, in which both political parties heartily joined in making a grand success. The Whigs gave the HARRISON BALL at the Washington House, on Tuesday, February 9, 1841; while the Democrats commemorated the exit of their President with the VAN BUREN BALL, at the Rockford House, on Wednesday, 3d of March, 1841, at 4 o'clock p. m. It is passing strange that I should have preserved my tickets of invitation to both these balls, to reproduce them which I now do verbatim et literatim, fifty years afterwards. The Harrison ticket was printed at the office of the *Rock River Express;* the Van Buren ticket at the *Rockford Star* office, and both are bronzed.

The ball room at the Washington House was superior to anything at that time in the State, and for many years after. It was 20 by 60 feet, with two sets of joice, the upper set supporting the floor, of ash lumber, and elastic like a spring-board. I have never seen its equal for a dancing party. As illustrative of the absence of all animosity between the two late political antagonists, the desire that each should make a grand success, my father, rock-rooted, hardshell Democrat as he was, at the request of the Millers who built and kept the Washington House, and who had little or no experience in affairs of this kind, took charge of preparing the meats and table arrangements for the banquet, and my mother of the pastry and table decorations.

The ball came off as per program, the house being packed.

Harrison Ball.

"On with the Dance, let Joy be unconfined!
No sleep till morn, when Youth and Pleasure meet,
To chase the glowing hours with flying feet."

THE undersigned solicit the company of

Mr. John H. Thurston and Lady,

at a BALL to be held in honor of the natal-day of our President-Elect, at the WASHINGTON HOUSE, in Rockford, on Tuesday, February 9th, 1841.

MANAGERS.

OSGAR TAYLOR,
T. D. ROBERTSON, } Rockford.
ALONZO PRATT,
J. C. WATERMAN, Newburg;
D. M. BRISTOL, Belvidere;
D. J. BUNDY, Beloit;

J. C. SCOTT,
JOHN GAIRNS,
CHARLES HALL,
C. WATERMAN, Sycamore;
F. BUSS, Pleasant Grove;
HORATIO HUNT, Freeport.

Inspired by the grand success of their recent political foes, the Democrats determined to surpass them if possible, or in any event to have their administration go out in a blaze of glory. This was the ticket.

EARLY DAYS IN ROCKFORD.

VAN BUREN BALL.

"HONOR TO WHOM HONOR IS DUE."

The Company of John A. Thurston and Lady is respectfully requested at a Ball to be given by **D. HOWELL,** *at the* Rockford House, ROCKFORD, *Winnebago County, Ill., on Wednesday, 3d March, 1841, at 4 o'clock P. M., in honor of the able and enlightened administration of* Martin Van Buren.

D. S. HAIGHT, J. TRULY SHALER, C. I. HORSMAN, CHAS. CONRAD, R. S. MALONY, L. A. DOOLITTLE, H. WATERMAN, B. F. LAWRENCE, A. R. DODGE, L. P. SANGER,	} Rockford. } Belvidere. } Ottawa.	J. M. STRODE, M. O. WALKER, THOMPSON CAMPBELL, A. L. HOLMES, H. McKENNEY, L. P. CRARY,	J. C. GOODHUE, CHA'S LATIMER. H. W. LOOMIS, F. BIERER. } Chicago. } Madison, Milwaukee. F. ALDRICH, W.M. JACKSON } Galena. JEHIEL DAY } Joliet. } Coral. } Daysville.
JNO. D. WINTERS,	} Elizabeth.	JNO. M. FINCH,	} Stephenson.
JAMES LYBRAND,	} Monroe.	JULIUS M. WARREN,	} Warrenville.
JOSEPH NAPIER,	} Naperville.	JAMES CAMPBELL,	} Aurora.
HENRY MAYARD,	} St. Charles.	DAVID DUNHAM,	} Geneva. WM. KIMBALL } Elgin
CHAS. WATERMAN, TIMOTHY WELLS, WM. B. SHELDON, S. STOUGHTON, M. BEAUBIEN, JR., S. M. LAYTON, H. W. LEFFINGWELL, MERRIL E. MACK,	} Sycamore. } Janesville. } Kiskwakee. } Pecatonic.	WM. WILKISON, D. B. McKENNEY, DAVID NOGGLE CHA'S DURGIN, GEO. F. AMES, S. P. HYDE, H. THURSTON, JNO. W. DYER	} Dixon. } Beloit. } Amesville. } Harlem J. R. HOWE, L.O.CROCKER ORRIS CROSBY, H. SHATTUCK. R. F. HOYT, JNO. STEELE, T. H. T. MOSS, W. W.FULLER, } Freeport } Ohio Grove } Newburg. } Oregon City.
MOSES M. STRONG,	} Mineral Point.	A. BROWN,	} Grand De Tour.
H. S. HALL,	} Millford.	THOS. COON,	} Winnebago. D. A. BLAKE, } Roscoe.
JNO. PLATT,	} Trask's Ferry.	RUFUS COLTON,	} Coltonville.

The celebration came off as per programme in the early evening of the third of March, 1841. Doct. Orris Crosby of Ohio Grove, Boone county, the oldest Democrat present, and Miss Mary A. Barrett of Harlem, fiance of the writer, the youngest democrat in the house, opened the ball.

The doctor, who was spare, and six feet or more in hight, was clad in a blue broadcloth swallow-tailed coat with brass buttons, in the style of the twenties, an immense rolling collar extending up the back of his head, trousers four inches shorter than are now worn, red stockings and calfskin pumps, started the revelry with his favorite figure of Upper Reel; and the way the old Democrat pigeon-winged as he swung corners and balanced to partner, was the envy of us youngsters. Down the outside one or more bars of music as the room available would allow and return; down the center and return between the two lines of dancers; cast off one couple; swing your partner and the opposite lady; swing your partner and the lady at the head of the set; balance to and swing your partner and repeat the figure. In after years, Mary used to say she was in mortal fear during this dance the old Democrat would trip her up while executing the more elaborate steps in his pigeon-winging.

In my scrap book I find a clipping from the *Chicago Democrat*, in which "Long John Wentworth" makes mention of this ball.

"A VALUABLE PRESENT.—We ought long ago to have returned our thanks to the landlord of the Rockford House and to the party which assembled there at the Democratic ball, on the 3d, for a large box of choice selections from the table provided for that occasion; but the recent excitements have kept our mind in another direction. Among them we would mention the following, viz:

1 Roast Turkey,	1 Bottle Champagne,
1 Roast Chicken,	1 Large Sugar Rooster,
1 Pyramid of Cake,	1 Cranberry Pie,
6 Large slices of Cake, of different varieties.	
1 Mince Pie,	About 2 ℔s. Alamode Beef,
About 3 ℔s. Rock River Cheese.	

And any quantity of little fixings embracing lozenges, candies, tarts, &c., &c.

We would not forget to mention, however, a small flag, said to be carried by whatever lady happened to dance at the head, with the inscription—'Ex-President Van Buren, Col. Wentworth, and Rock River Democracy;' nor the many printed compliments selected by this and that person as appropriate to our condition and desert in life. One writes 'twenty Mary's were present on the occasion, besides some who were just as pretty, though they went by another name.' We say, give us Rockford yet for remembering editors."

For a decade and more afterwards these two balls were mentioned by the participants, whenever they desired to refer to a big thing in the terpsichorean line.

CHAPTER X.

First Brick House on the West Side—First White Children Born in the County—Mrs Haight's Sister—The Charivari—Selden M. Church and Mary Preston—Their Wedding Turn-Out—Isaiah Lyon and Mary Hitchcock—Their Wedding Reception—The De'il Himself Loose—Pandemonium—A Swinette—The Army Trail—Indian Camp—The Best Road on Earth---Prairie Grass---Red-Root---Massasauguas---The Hoosier Whip---Alexander Miller in 1838---Fishing---Waterfowl---Pigeons---Deer---Jake Kite---His Rifle---Snuffs a Candle---To Oregon in 1845---Sylvester Scott's Mother Shoots a Deer--Sylvester's Account of the Exploit.

The first brick house on the west side was built by Doct. George Haskell and Isaiah Lyon on the northwest corner of State and Main streets, in the fall of 1838. The cellar was dug in August, and during the fall and winter the building was finished and occupied—two stories, with store and offices below and hall above; the hall being used by the Baptist church for religious services. When the lot was staked out, Mr. Harvey H. Silsby, who is a house joiner and was then in the employ of Doct. Haskell, persuaded him to set the building back six feet from the line on both fronts. I have these items from Mr. Silsby in person, and the fine appearance of the north side of State street is owing to his good judgment at that early day. This building was quite generally known as the Winnebago House. Some time in the early fifties, it was refitted and first opened as a hotel by the late Isaac N. Cunningham, who made it one of the most popular hostelries in the country.

It is stated, I think, in R. P. Porter's history of this county, that George E. Dunbar, now of Memphis, Tenn., was the first white child born in Winnebago county. I supposed that was the case, and have a faint recollection of so informing Porter. Some few years ago Mr. Dunbar called at my house, when I showed him a memoranda in pencil which my wife had obtained through the late Miss Jane Jackson, and which Mr. Dunbar said was correct. Although faint, this memoranda, which is in the chirography of a lady, is readily deciphered with a glass. It is as follows, and is here inserted as a matter of record : " February, 1836, Mrs. John B. Long introduced the first female child in Winnebago Co., which was Melissa J. The first male child born was Ogden Hance, in what is now Pecatonica township." Miss Jackson was a sister of Mr. Dunbar's mother. Mr. Dunbar gave to my wife a cabinet photo of himself, which is now in the possession of Mrs. E. P. Catlin of 302 South First street.

This seems an opportune time in which to make a record of another early settler who has been incorrectly reported in the local press. Quite recently I saw a statement in one of the town papers, that Mrs. Haight's sister, a Miss Carey, was one of the persons present at the first religious meeting held in this county in 1835, at the house of Germanicus Kent. It goes to show how difficult it is to accurately remember names for fifty years, and more. The early settler who gave the item to the reporter is mistaken as to her name. I was present at the marriage of this young woman in Haight's log cabin. Her name was Abigal Stearns. I quote from the record of marriages in the county clerk's office:

"April 5th, 1837, Samuel I. Corey was married to Miss Abigal Stearns. Certified. W. E. DUNBAR, J. P."

Writing of marriage and giving in marriage, brings to mind a custom adopted by the youngsters among the early settlers, which they borrowed from the French who peopled Kaskaski at a remote day—THE CHARIVARI. If the fellow upon this momentous event in his life didn't "come down," he must abide the consequences. On the other hand, if on the evening of May 20, 1845, (I get the date from my scrap book,) the day when Selden M. Church and Mary Preston were joined in marriage, a charivari had been attempted, it wouldn't have been a healthy undertaking, as the party would have been summarily squelched. At 1 p. m. sharp that day, I drove up to the front of the Rockford House with "Black Lucy," the handsomest horse in town, hitched in the shafts of an open buggy with wood axles, basswood dash, seat upholstered with a buffalo robe and clean harness—the best in town—from the livery of Tyler & Thurston, which equipage I had in charge for the occasion and handed the reins to the Judge. He was followed as he drove off by the benedictions of the assembly. We had no shoes to throw after them, as they were required for personal use, and rice had not yet come in vogue; but God bless you's and our best wishes did follow in the wake of the disappearing vehicle. The bars of the Rockford and Washington Houses were open that afternoon and evening to all the acquaintances of the newly wedded couple, and were patronized to a moderate extent only; one cigar, the flavor moistened by a single drink sufficed.

Isaiah Lyon and Mary Hitchcock were married March 31, 1841. I also get this from my scrap-book. In fact I am largely indebted to this scrap-book which has been filled from time to time in past years without thought of ever using it for my present work. Miss Mary

Hitchcock was a most popular young lady, as were all ladies at the time, married or unmarried; but Isaiah Lyon, her fiance, and Jonathan Hitchcock ("Old Funds") her father, were promising subjects for a charivari, even had they "come down like a thousand of brick," which they failed to do in any way, and were given such a charivari as eclipsed all previous or succeeding efforts in that line, having as participants parties in all ranks of life. My memory has recently been refreshed by a participant who was then, and is still a member in good standing of the Baptist church to which Lyon then belonged, and to which he adhered through life. The charivari came off in front of the house No. 107 North First street, now occupied by Doct. E. J. Johnson as a residence. This house was built by Jonathan Hitchcock, and was then new. The Baptist brother tells me in effect like this: "I had a hand in working up the charivari. Lyon had played several tricks on me during the summer before, and boy-like, I wanted satisfaction, and got in my work to bring it about. Charles Oliver worked it on the west side, and 'Mel' Turner came in to let us know when Lyon came home from his wedding trip, so we could hold our concert the evening of their return." My own particular duty for the occasion was to prepare fire-balls, and to gather material for bonfires.

The concert came off as per programme, the weather proving admirable for the purpose. One fellow had a large dry goods box with the cover off, which he planted immediately in front of the house, and with a piece of scantling well resined, which he rapidly drew across the edges of this box, produced an unearthly screech as though the De'il himself had broke loose. The bonfires being well started, the Baptist brother disguised with a buffalo robe fastened about his waist and projecting well above his head, carrying a horse fiddle (a rattle) as big as he could swing, headed the motely procession. Horns, tin pans, cow-bells, drums, bars of steel, guns and every conceivable thing to make a noise were brought into requisition. Pandemonium wasn't a circumstance. Each man and boy on his own hook, and each striving to outdo the other.

During all this time the family in the house stood at the front windows apparently enjoying the scene which was brilliantly illuminated, as well as those outside. Finally the performers on wind instruments became so exhausted they couldn't raise a squeak, when Nicholas ("Nick") Smith, a carpenter on the west side, and a genius from New Jersey, produced a new instrument of torture which he then and there dubbed a "Swinette." Followed by the regiment, he appeared on the scene, each man carrying under his arm as large a shoat as he could well handle—there were lots of 'em sleeping around every manure pile in town—while grasping the muzzle of the animal in his hand, when he produced a high or a low note by opening or shutting its mouth. When the pig became partially exhausted they'd carry him into the bar-room and "tune up the Swinette," as Nick said, "with a glass of whisky. If pandemoneum reigned brfore, it was doubly intensified now with each pig squealing in all the notes of the gamut. When the supply of small hogs gave out they caught the large ones, dragging them by the hind legs as long as they could utter a sound, and so ended the most noted charivari party of northern Illinois.

When I arrived and for nearly two years after, the roads were termed trails, and between prominent points almost invariably followed the Indian trail. General Scott's army trail made in 1832, when he followed Black Hawk's band to the head waters of the Rock, passed through the first ward. Stephen Mack, the Indian trader at the mouth of the Pecatonica was the guide. This trail met the river bank above the town at the dry run which is now bridged on North Second street, near the residence of H. H. Hamilton. It followed the bank of the river to the first creek above the town, when the wagon trail turned east on the south side of the creek and crossed the stream at the identical spot where the first bridge over the creek is now located. On the small piece of bottom land at this crossing, where it is surrounded on the north side by a high bluff, a permanent winter Indian camp of some half dozen tepees had been located; the site of each tepee being plainly designated in 1837 by marks of fire and a low ring of earth. This was an excellent location, as there was shelter, wood, water, and an abundance of cottonwood along the creek for the ponies. The army trail crossed the bluff and met the Indian trail near the railroad track at the foot of the Big Bottom, where it followed the Indian trail through the center of the prairie, crossing Willow creek eighty rods west of the bridge on the center road. The Indian trail was right beside—west—of the wagon trail and could plainly be seen for half a mile. These trails were as straight from point to point as a man would walk, and always chose the best location.

A wagon trail on the prairie when it has worn through the sod, is the best road on earth in dry weather, being as smooth as a billiard table and elastic to the tread of a horse, without a stone in sight for mile after mile. As the travel was light and almost exclusively with two horses, a wagon trail like that between Rockford and Beloit had a comb of sod in the center on which the grass grew freely. This was the case on the Big Bottom as late as 1846. The prairie grass grew in small bunches or tufts, the blades of the grass having sharp edges which cut out the leather on the toes of a pair of boots rapidly, unless protected with a strip of tin tacked to the sole of the boot, a custom almost universal. There was a plant on the prairie called redroot from the color of the root which was nearly as dark as blood. The plant was about a foot high at maturity; the roots being from half an inch to four inches in diameter, and tough as hickory, while being much more durable in the earth. These large roots would frequently bring a breaking team to a stand-still. There were lots of rattlesnakes (massasauguas) on the Big Bottom, but usually of smaller size than those found in the sloughs. In breaking the sod the "land" was laid off from six to ten rods wide depending on its length and the size of the team. As the sod was turned—usually two to two and a half inches thick—the snakes retreated to the center and were killed by the driver's whip.

The Hoosier ox whip deserves special mention, the size of the instrument depending on the muscle of its owner. I've seen a man control a team of eight yokes of oxen, the leaders and wheelers only being fairly broken, with one of these whips. He would stand on the near side of the team about twenty-five feet away from the center of the line, and strike each ox within four inches of the spot where he intended to hit him, bringing blood at every blow. The stalk was from ten to fourteen feet long, with a lash of raw-hide half as long again, and a snapper of buckskin, the report being a sharp crack quite equal to a rifle.

In my scrap book I find an article cut from the "*Forest and Stream,*" many years ago, which I recognize as from the pen of Alexander Miller, who returned to Pittsburgh, Pa., in 1838, and was subsequently joined there by his elder brother Jacob ("Jake") B., where they became one of the leading legal firms in the city. It opens the subject of game in this locality in better language than I have at command, and I make use of it:

"At the time of my arrival in Rockford two rival villages were competing for supremacy, and for the location of the county court house and other public buildings, one on the east and the other on the west bank of Rock river. The proposer of the proposed site on the east bank was one Haight; of the west bank the firm of Kent & Brinkerhoff. After a long and angry controversy, the county seat was finally located on the west side of the river."

"At first I was completely enamored of the country; the beautiful rolling prairies were studded all over with wild flowers, which grew most luxuriantly. One week the prairie would be all over white when a certain white flower would predominate; a fortnight afterwards it would be all blue when another flower would predominate, and so on throughout the whole summer, when each successive flower in its season would be in the ascendant, thus giving to us in regular succession all the various colors of the rainbow, between early summer and autumn. My stay at Rockford was about six months, and having comparatively little else to do, I passed my time principally in the pleasures of hunting and fishing, in both of which that summer I was eminently successful as any other novice might have been. It was about six years after the Black Hawk war, but even at that time, on traversing the prairie on the east side of the river, I could discern plainly and follow easily the track of our army, which marched along the river against Black Hawk and his army of Indian warriors, the wheels of the heavily laden baggage wagons having cut through the sod of the prairie. The country was sparsely populated, East Rockford was a small village, and West Rockford a much smaller one; of course there were few sportsmen, but there were some. Nearly all the pioneers were husbandmen, intent on digging a living out of old mother earth. As to game, the prairies were filled with pinnated grouse, the thickets with ruffed grouse; and as for Rock river, it was literally alive with fish of the most magnificent proportions and of the greatest variety. Deer were abundant, as were wild geese and ducks in their seasons."

"For some time after my arrival in Rockford I amused myself by fishing with rod and line, killing all the bass and pickerel I desired. One evening after finishing my afternoon sport, and about to start for the village, I discovered lying on the bank a huge fishing pole, which had evidently been used by some stalwart rustic. The butt was a part of a hickory sapling, to which was spliced a long pole. It was of immense weight, considering the use for which it was intended. I affixed a line to this pole, baited it with a minnow, and fastening the butt firmly in the ground and covering it with great heavy stones, I threw the baited line into the river. On the next morning I returned and found that I had hooked a monster fish in the night; the butt of the rod was sticking firmly in the ground where I had placed it, the rod was broken at the point where it was so strongly spliced, and the fish had made good its escape. At the time it was believed that this was the work of one of what we then called the Mississippi catfish, for it was supposed at that time that such immense catfish as were sometimes found in Rock river could only be grown in the Mississippi."

"During the summer a friend of the writer's constructed a drop line, or as it is called in this section of country, a 'night line.' Attached to it were perhaps forty or fifty hooks, which being baited, the line was stretched across the river in the evening. The next morning my friend went to the river to raise his night line and to witness the success of his enterprise, when to his great surprise he discovered that the fish had literally carried off the whole line, and he never saw hook or thread of it afterwards. This was the first and last night line set in Rock river during my sojourn in that country. And yet another mode was resorted to in order to capture the fish in Rock river, which I am ashamed to relate, for it was so destructive and so very unlike the true sportsman. Verily, I believe that if old Isaac Walton had been present he would have hung every one of us up to a tree. Opposite the town of Rockford, and above the rapids, the river bottom was smooth and free from all obstructions. We procured a seine of very considerable length, by a single draw of which we could supply the whole population of the town with fish to last them several days. The modus operandi was as follows: The seine was placed on the stern of a skiff, one man plied the oars while another would drive the skiff up stream, thence toward the middle, and thence down and around until we would land on the shore a little distance below the starting point; the seine was then drawn by parties at either end slowly toward the shore, and when within twenty or thirty feet of the bank the excitement began. Such a kicking and jumping and splashing! There was the monster Mississippi catfish, weighing from fifty to eighty pounds, the huge sturgeon from three to four feet long, the 'buffalo' weighing as high as eighty pounds, 'red-horse' and other fish without number. But we did not destroy all these. The tastes of the then residents of Rockford were very refined and delicate, and the three last named fish—bass, pickerel, and 'red-horse'—were the only ones used. All the rest were consigned to the river again."

Another unsportsmanlike mode of capturing fish which Mr. Miller does not mention, was spearing, in which art nearly all the native frontiersmen were experts. There was a small bayou just above State street on the east side, and at the mouth of Kent's creek on the west side, where liberal supplies were obtained of muskallonge, bass and pickerel with a spear, the fisherman usually operating with a canoe. I've seen a man stand on the gunwales of a light canoe-built for passenger service, and with a setting pole used on one side only of the craft, set it up over the rapids as fast as one could walk on the shore.

Having never shot a game bird previous to my arrival in Rockford, the vast quantity of feathered game which I saw migrating northward in the spring of 1837, excited my unbounded surprise and admiration. Swans, geese, ducks, and all the various species of water fowl followed each other in endless succession up the valley of the river, while sand hill cranes, eagles, and other large birds of which no one seemed to have a knowledge, were navigating the air. The passenger pigeons made a roost in the timber east of what is now Marengo, in numbers sufficient to break down the limbs of trees. These birds when traveling to and from their feeding grounds passed over the little hamlet in countless millions, while "the woods were full of them." Our party were well provided with fire arms, a ten bore single barrel shot gun—the barrel forty inches long—being a part of my special baggage. The wood ducks raised their young in the groves immediately about the town and all the game so abundant in after years were seen, with the exception of quail; there were none here when I came. They followed the immigration, and were here in countless numbers from 1844 to 1854. Deer were abundant. The first I saw was early in April, 1837, in the woods near the place where the State road meets the timber, where I encountered a drove of nine. The edges of the timber nearly all the way from Cedar Bluff cemetery to the Kishwaukee, were a dense thicket where the deer could hide, and the few here who knew how to hunt them rarely failed to get a shot. The Mulford estate was a capital hunting ground for deer and ruffed grouse, as was the valley of Keith's creek. The prairie chickens multiplied more than ten-fold in five years, owing to the better food supply, as well as the ignorance of most of the new comers of the art of wing-shooting over a pointer, and the fact that the native western pioneer had a supreme contempt for the scatter gun. The most expert deer hunter I ever met was "Jake" Kite, who lived with "Old Spoors" on a claim in what is now Guilford, and for many years after owned and occupied by Solomon Wheeler. A few weeks after my arrival, I met Jake one Saturday afternoon in Bundy & Goodhue's store, as he sauntered into the room with his rifle on his shoulder and carefully set it in a corner of the room. Twenty minutes after he was reasonably mellow; just sufficient to be talkative and good natured. The gun was a pill lock, the hammer when cocked standing at a right angle with the barrel, an indentation in the side of the barrel smeared over with tallow holding the pill, and carried a larger ball than was usual at that time; it was as quick as the modern breech loader. There wasn't a particle of bright metal about it; the muzzle sight of white bone fashioned by himself, while the rear sight was a straight bar with a slight V in the center. My boyish curiosity caused me to take the rifle in hand to examine the lock, having never before seen one like it. "Take care, bub," said Jake, "she's loaded," and he took it himself. "Where's the cap?" "She don't use airy cap," and from one of the pockets of his hunting shirt he produced a quill partly filled with what I supposed to be onion seed, and explained the method of priming the arm, and that the tallow smeared over the priming was to keep out moisture. "Wait till I get our rifle," and I soon handed him a finely finished piece, gorgeous in its silver mountings and engraving. Jake examined it with the eye of a connoisseur. "She's right smart, but them trimmings ain't worth shucks." "Is she loaded?" "Yes, all but the cap." "Lets see you shoot her," and I followed him outside. "There bub, d'ye see the black spot on that tree?" (pointing to one just below the Rockford House,) "let's see you spile it." Taking the wiping stick in my left hand and using it for a rest while I knelt on one knee, I made a line shot four inches above the mark, much to my delight. "She's sighted for 18 to 20 rods, bub, you must draw a finer sight." "Now Jake, you try it," and he did. The muzzle of the rifle wabbled as Jake's body swayed to and fro under the influence of the liquor, but at the instant of the explosion he was as rigid as a statue. I ran to the mark, Jake following leisurely. I could find no trace of the bullet on the tree. "Look *in* the mark, bub," said Jake, and to my surprise I found the bullet hole there. Under Jake's instructions I learned during the summer to draw a "fine sight," and with a dead rest, could make a fair showing with Jake himself in shooting at a mark.

One of Jake's feats was to snuff a candle in the evening with a rifle ball, and the more intense the darkness the more easily he accomplished it. A lighted candle is placed in a small box with one side removed and stepping off thirty paces from the front of the light, Jake rarely failed to extingush it. He explained it to me by saying that when he saw the mark, the front and rear sights, he pulled the trigger. It simply requires a quick finger on the trigger, and resolution not to pull until the three objects are in line. As the country became more populous, Jake Kite and kindred spirits were the first to migrate west. They could see the smoke from a neighboring chimney contaminating the air, and were filled with a feeling of suffocation. Early in the spring of 1845, "Old Spoors," Jake Kite, a Mr. Jolly, with others from this vicinity, formed part of the advanced guard to Oregon. Mr. Jolly was not less than seventy years old when he started with a team of four mules, which he drove there from the foot of the Big Bottom to Oregon.

While making notes and getting material together for a chapter relating to the game so abundant at an early day, I remembered that Sylvester Scott's mother once killed a deer with a rifle in the immediate vicinity of their log cabin in what is now Guilford, where she resided with her young family. I wrote to Sylvester for details of the event, to which he promptly responded. His reply was so characteristic, his pen pictures of pioneer life so true to the reality at the time of which he writes, that I wrote a second letter asking permission to publish his account of the deer killing, to which he readily assented. As I did not feel warranted in so doing, or like to make any change in the style of his description, I herewith append the latter, verbatim et literatim:

FRIEND THURSTON.

Yours of the 12, at hand and finds me busily engaged in nursing the Grippe. I think I seldom have passed a more uneasy night than last night. am a little better to-day. but that is not saying much.

> For its cough and then sneeze,"
> The most of the day;
> Without comfort and grace.
> "In, the varied display;
> While you feel so disgusted
> You'r tempted to Swear
> That you do not feel better
> Mid'st THIS TERRIBLE TEAR—

We have had our share of colds," Grippe" and Hog Cholare," but are able to be about: and I could relish a nice piece of Veneson," this morning "most Royally" mons" Thurston". Botsford," Says that Homer himself would not Recognized his own Poetry, after Syl" Scott coppied it. Rther hard on Scott, but" I will try and tell you my verison of the Deer" Killing" Nevertheless. . . . .

It was in the fall of 38th to the best of my recollection," that the event of Shooting that Deer occured. "Frosted" out of "Cold" Cattaraug; (as this co" in the State of N Y. Was called"; from which we Emigrated to this co; We moved by Horse and wagon," taking us five weeks to accomplish the journey. our Route was first to Buffalo". here we crossed the Niaggary River" at Black Rock" into Cannady; then to the Falls; "from here to Detroit," then to Michigan City;' then around the Lake to Chicago," and from Chicago" to the present co of Winnebago. Ill.

Their was more "hundred cent "ers" then," than Millienaires" in this co. and you can rest assured," We were not running over with the nessessaries, of life" needed upon this muudame Sphere. a few ℔s of Hoosier Hog", (as we used to call them) was a luxary much coveted," and it answered a two-fold purpose," to Sop our Jenny Cake," in; and Lubricate the Spider," to Keep it from adhering unto—it. This much desired Article, consisted of, first," a Rine about half an inch thick." then a layer of gristly fat" of about the same thickness. after this came a succession of layers, of uncertain make up," terminating with the Ribs'; and insid requiremants;" "but with all its Swineish peculiarities", it answered a purpose; and was successfully applied wherever necessity directed. But "there was other delicasies coveted by the Pioneer of these days", these were made up of Game of various kinds so abundant in those days. My Father" then a man in the prime of life," had little time to Hunt. and when he did," it would be only a few moments" at Sun Set," to pick a few Pheasants from their pearch for the night; or drop a Wild-Goose upon the Wing'; or a Prairie Chichen that ventnred to near his place of Labor.

About a ¼ of a mile from our log Cabin was a slough" where the wild Grass grew abundant," and we had mowed it to procure our Winters Hay. it was in Sept or Oct. and the young grass had started up fresh and green" and offered a sweet morsel to the numerous droves of Deer that roamed freely over Wood and prairie," in those Early day's. Mother was the Daughter of a Hunter. although Born in Cape May. co N J. and at one time the owner of a valuable propperty in this co. but as the hard times "after the War of 1812 came" he Mortgaged all to Jacob," Rigeway". of Phil'a. and moved into Penn". upon some of the tributary Streams of the Susquhanneh River, to engage in Rafting timber for the Market South. a five year sojourn in this place, gave Mother a lesson in the killing of large Game. Deer " Elk," Bear. Wolves & Panthers " hovered about their Wild Retreat;" and many a fine Specimen fell " by the hand of David Johnson." in those Wild Regions of the Allegania Mountains ; and it was here she learned to use her Fathers "Pet " Rifle, (and which is still kept by my Brother Daniel. Scott," of "Guilford:

It was at the close of a beautiful Autumn day. the Pheasants could be seen browsing on the tree tops " and Numerous flocks of Geese. and Ducks were flying past on their Way to River; and Pond. The Squirel was nimbly running from tree to tree," and men was engaged in our Evening Chorus " so well remember by the hunter of those Days.

Mother," told Brother and I. she would go and see if she could not kill a Deer. leaving our two Sisters with us; (the youngest but a few months old) she shouldered the Pet Rifle," and started for the meadow. But a short time elapsed," before the sharp crack of a Rifle rang out upon the Evening air," and shortly after the Schrill voice of a Woman, calling for some one to help her. She had droped the Deer "—a fine Doe," and it was struggling frantically about," "and a mortal fear Struck her, that " it migbt get away. She had no hunting knife; and quickly reloading She fired a final shot into its head, that soon put all fear aside. the Scene of the shooting, was about 100 rods E. of the Old log School House," where Cirus. Jenks. Kept School. You will remember this. Soloman. Greely " my Wife's Father; lived about the same distance North. upon hearing the Rifle, and Mother calling for help, he cought a Butcher Knife and hastened to the rescue. the Deer was silent. Mother was excitedly watching the game, and the happiest Woman in America," just then. Father soon returned from the City of Forest's, "learned the facts," and the Deer was soon at the Cabin, and Dressed," cut up," and more than one Family feasted upon "Venison Steak that Evening.

Those were days of trials and happiness mingled together. most of the Dear ones " so "sacred to memory have gone to the land of Spirits. a few linger behind; but time flyes on Wings and we to will soon follow. as I write these recollections, my Dear " Mother comes to my side," and whispers " it is Well," my Son," "God Ruleth."

I have read your articles with Interest. they are very correct " as far as I remember. Respectfully yours as Ever.

SYLVESTER. SCOTT.

CHAPTER XI.

Deer Hunting in 1837—Buck-Fever—Quail by the Wagon Load—Price per Dozen—First Fresh Oysters—Quail Suppers—John Frink and The Hunters—Immense Numbers of Prairie Chickens—Three Hundred Shot Over One Dog—Thirteen Down—From Glasgow to Rockford to Shoot—Bird Dogs—Charley Pratt of Freeport—Seventeen Turkeys—Ike Stoneman's Tavern—A Glass of Gin—Tut Baker, Charley Waterman, Seth Farwell and Fred. Strocky of Freeport—Web-Foot Rabbit—Poetry (?)—Various Game Birds—Conclusion—Acknowledgments.

I do not recall a single instance where one of the town boys in 1837-8 succeeded in securing a deer, although they often shot at them. Their usual hunting ground was from near the Richardson brick yard to the Mulford estate and south of that point. Most of the youngsters among the new comers became quite expert in shooting at a mark with a rifle, but at game in the woods, and more particularly at deer, they were afflicted with "buck-fever," and while it is possible they may have wounded one, I never knew a deer to be brought in as a trophy. In the fall of 1837, a hunt was organized and sides chosen, each one selected having the privilege of providing a substitute. John Miller, father of the Miller boys, was captain of one side, and Henry Thurston of the other, both of them being too old and infirm to participate personally in the sport. Jake Kite was my father's substitute, who brought in the only deer killed that day. Jake's relation to me of his successful shot is as vivid in memory as though it were yesterday. The locality was near the scene of Mrs. Scott's exploit. Jake was cautiously passing through a dense thicket when he heard the deer coming and dropped beside a log. As the animal approached he mounted the log and called out "halt!" The deer stopped instantly, and raising its head Jake could see the outline of his horns and neck through the brush, when he shot him through the neck. Following the trail for half a mile, he observed the deer began to stagger, when he sent out his dog, who soon had him down. This dog never left his heels except when ordered. "But Jake," said I, "Why didn't you put the dog on the trail at first?" "He'd a run five miles bub, if I'd a done that." My own experience in hunting deer is not flattering. The first trial I made was late in the fall of 1839. There came a fall of snow and I started for the head-waters of Willow Creek, armed with a single barrel ducking gun, heavily charged with buck shot. Within half a mile of the present locality of the Scotch church, I ran into a drove of five, and while a fine doe stood about forty paces away for not less than two minutes, gazing and snuffing at a large bush which concealed me, I stood there with my heart in my throat, utterly unconscious I held a gun in my hands, and my mission that day was to kill a deer. A more clear case of "buck fever" was never developed.

As previously stated, there were no quail here when I first came, but they followed the immigration closely. From 1844 to '52, they were here in countless numbers. Quite recently I heard a fellow— not a sportsman—boast of potting thirteen at one shot. I am happy to say I never murdered them after that fashion, but with dog and gun gave the little beauties a chance for life. During the winter of 1852-3, the season the railroad track first reached Rockford, quail were brought in barrels by the wagon load from Stephenson county and shipped east. After they acquired a commercial value they diminished rapidly in numbers. This, with a few severe winters, has in this locality caused them to have become extinct in recent years. In the early forties, quail were used in winter as a substitute for oysters in making soup. The country boys caught them in traps; dressed and brought them in to barter for ammunition at a price not to exceed eighteen cents per dozen. We cooked them in a chafing-dish with an alcohol lamp, making with butter and spices, a most delicious dish. The first fresh oysters received in the town was about the first of February, 1847. They were brought in the stage from Detroit. The incident is forcibly impressed on my memory from the fact there was no alcohol in the town, and Goodhue's whisky being a temperance drink, wouldn't burn in the lamp, which I finally filled and used with hot lard, though it smoked like blazes. Andrew Lovejoy, who was the chef, pronounced the bivalves to be the famed "Shrewsbury oysters" of the Fulton Market in New York.

We had most delicious quail suppers in the early winter months. Ah! if I were set back forty-five years—a boy once more—I could appreciate the situation, for it never occurred to us the game would become nearly or quite extinct in our day. In November and December we went out in the afternoon in the immediate vicinity of the town for quail. On the east side, skirting the grove from the intersection of State and Kishwaukee streets to Buckbee's addition; on the west side, from the fair grounds up the creek to the edge of the timber and around to the river. The surplus not required for the supper was distributed among friends. I never knew an instance where feathered game was sold by the sportsman. In the evening we put up the shutters and locked the store door. The dogs knew this was preliminary to dressing the game and were on the alert. We skinned the game invariably, each dog sitting in front of his master expecting the titbits—heads, hearts, lungs, etc.; when by chance or design, he gave another dog a morsel, there was a fight instanter. While the game was being dressed, others of the party were on a foraging expedition for bread. Many a time the good housewife, when looking for the staff of life, while preparing the matutinal meal, has discovered it had disappeared in the most unaccountable way, while at the same time her life companion had no appetite for breakfast, neither could he imagine how the bread and sometimes the butter also, had taken flight. We had a gridiron specially made with long legs and handle, to fit the door of the box stove in the store; with a head of cabbage, a large box of sardines to made cole-slaw; butter, bread, vinegar, etc., a large platter on which to serve the game, and appetites sharpened by the exercise, the feast which followed was fit for the Gods; the dogs meanwhile whining with excitement, each one keeping close beside his master and asking in plain dog language for his share of the rations. In those days the New York and Boston drummers came west before the close of navigation, remaining in this region making collections during the winter. These fellows could always be relied upon at such occasions, for all the sardines and champagne we chose to make way with; this last commodity being an indulgence our finances would not allow.

There was no town in the state outside of Chicago, where there was so many wing shots and trained bird dogs, as there was in Rockford. The stage passengers dined here, and fifty miles away were told during the shooting season, they would have a game dinner at Rockford. Mr. John Frink of the stage firm of Frink & Walker, a most able business man, was disgusted with the hunters he encountered here when making his trips over the line; characterizing us as a set of loafers, and the mass of them were as a matter of fact. Mr. Frink said those he met in Chicago were conversing of the crop, and future prices for wheat. In Galena, it was the out-put and price for lead; when he got to Rockford, about all he heard was "my dog stood with his tail on a dead level with his nose, while Jim's dog backed with his tail in the air," when another fellow would remark, "my dog's tail has become raw, and I'm plastering it with tar!" Mr. Martin O. Walker, the other partner of the firm, was as devoted to the gun as any of us, and when business called him here during the season, had his gun with him, to the great annoyance of Mr. Frink.

The number of pinnated grouse from 1846 to '50, in Winnobago, Boone, and Stephenson counties was prodigious. I've seen no account in recent years, where game birds were so plentiful, except the quail in San Diego county, California. I knew a company of nine, two only being expert shots, to go out in 1846, on Bonus Prairie, Boone county, who brought in over 300 chickens. As they had but one dog, they formed a line across a piece of low ground, traveling some twenty-five feet apart, and walked up the game for a mile and one-half. One familiar with the difficulty in finding a dead bird in grass knee high without the aid of a dog, may realize how many they actually shot. At 4 o'clock one afternoon in August 1848, Andrew Brown of the Rockford House and myself, went out on the west side, driving across the Garrison place to the Rockton road. Andrew dropped me about half a mile north of the corner now occupied by Dan. Carney, beside a piece of millet containing perhaps two acres, while he went on half a mile farther. After loading my gun—a double barrel—and adjusting game bag, powder flask and shot belt, I got over the fence, when the dog came to a point within ten feet of me. I shot thirteen there, having them all down at one time. In the meantime, Andrew hearing the fusillade, came back and put his dog in on the opposite side of the field. In less than one hour from the time I got out of the buggy, we had forty. On the Big Bottom just above the pickle farm now occupied by Mr. Snow, I've had nine down at one time with a single barrel gun. One day in August 1845, which was the year I first shot at game over a pointer, June & Turner's circus was to exhibit in the town; Judge Blackstone, who kept the Washington House, got me to take his two dogs the afternoon before the show arrived and secure a supply of chickens for the table. I left town after dinner with the dogs—pointers and well trained—drove to Milford, where "Len" Fountain joined me. We hunted from his wagon shop down stream on the river bottom, and when we arrived at the Dixon road, less than two miles, had fifty-two chickens and a bittern. I have known a party with seven guns to go out for an all day hunt on the low lands just below the mouth of the Killbuck, who had over a hundred birds stolen from their wagon which they never missed.

Some of the British army officers from Quebec, usually came to Chicago to shoot grouse during the season, finding an abundance of game within sight of the city. In 1849, two young gentlemen from Glasgow, Scotland, came here expressly to shoot grouse, finding quarters at the Rockford House; one of them hunting with Andrew Brown, the other with me. They both declared there was nothing like it in Europe, and also that our dogs were as well trained for the game we hunted, as any to be found in the old country. Of dogs, we never had any trouble to raise them, and they had all the stamina and hunting sense possible in the animal. I believe the offspring of trained parents will be better hunters, and more easily trained than if the case were otherwise, particularly so if the mother is hunted while carrying her young. My own favorite dog was a "dropper," and for all sorts of game, it would be difficult to find his equal. I could stand in the centre of an eighty acre lot and send him over any portion I chose by motion of my hand. He was a capital retriever, but in a hot day soon became heated. In my opinion for a bird dog only, the pointer is par excellence the king, and he may be trained for all game found in this latitude. Capin's dog would neither get over a fence or enter standing corn unless ordered. This dog would go around a field of corn, enter the grain and flush the birds, driving them towards his master. Old Charley Pratt, of Freeport, had a dog who would do this and more. This dog would take the trail of a deer, and if he found the animal hid in a thicket, would go around him and drive the deer in the direction of his master. Both these dogs were pointers.

A chapter on game in this locality at an early day, would certainly be incomplete which failed to mention Charley Pratt. He was the best wing shot I ever saw handle a gun, and could readily defeat the best of us whenever he set himself about it. He was a most accomplished musician, playing for balls about the country during the winter, and hunting in the summer and fall months, never performing any manual labor in his life. He once shot in the early fall, seventeen wild turkeys within two miles of Freeport. The birds were about two-thirds grown. He made the dog flush the flock, and then picked them up as though they were quail. He made his home at "Ike" Stoneman's tavern on Galena street, never paying a cent in money for the shelter given him for nearly two decades. Poor old Charley; the locomotive destroyed his only avocation in life, and he was unable to adapt himself to the changed conditions. He died in 1870, aged about 75 years, and the Freeport boys of early days, gave him a respectable burial. I last saw him one exceedingly warm morning in July 1868, when I met him at the foot of a flight of stairs on Stephenson street. It was evident he had just crawled out for the day, and had not finished his toilet, as bits of straw were distributed through his hair and beard. He grasped my hand with much emotion while tears coursed down his cheeks; we had not met in nearly a decade. "Charley," said I, "with your long residence in Freeport, your intimate acquaintance with its people, its highways and by-ways, have you any knowledge of a locality where we two may each procure a class of gin?" He sat down on the stairs behind him, dropped his head in deep meditation, finally turning up his kindly face to meet my gaze, when he replied, "I think I have," and started out on the street, bringing up in the basement of Fry's block.

We had an original song in the forties, common to Rockford and Freeport alike, taking in all the local events of the two towns, from old "Tut" Baker of Freeport, who did not know the alphabet, sitting in the corner of a worm fence, and wearing an immense pair of green spectacles while pretending to read a newspaper, and Charley Waterman and Seth Farwell, personating an old Irishman and woman from New Dublin, going to Fred Strocky's store on Stephenson street, to barter a basket of eggs for groceries. If there was anything in a fellow's past life, or like to happen in the near future which he would have preferred to keep shady, it was pretty sure sooner or later, to come out in this song. We were a jolly, happy crowd, intent on the pleasure of to-day with but little care for to-morrow, and what we did not get of the good things of this life within reach, was scarcely worth looking after. It would require the eloquence of Martin P. Sweet and the humor of Seth Farwell to do the subject justice; but presently, along came the locomotive, and all this and the game disappeared. Of this song which eventually grew to more than forty verses, all but a few have faded from my memory, the most of them pertaining to Stephenson county and Charley Pratt. It appears that before Charley came to Freeport, he was one of a company of market hunters who used to go to some of the islands in Lake Erie to shoot ducks. He once boarded where the housewife had been so unfortunate at some time in her life, as to have fallen into the fire and burned her face, making a scar which pulled one of her eyelids down, and she was popularly known as "old Tear Eye." There is some sort of weed grows there called "spice-foot," from which they used to make tea. She once gave him for supper what he supposed was stewed rabbit and he didn't discover it was a muskrat, until he got hold of one of the paws, which he held up and asked her "what sort of a rabbit that was?" to which she replied, "a web-foot rabbit." This event in his life was commemorated in the song, as were others. I presume the reason I remember these verses, is that Andrew Lovejoy and myself composed them with much trial and tribulation, while we were camped in the timber near the mouth of Richland creek above Freeport.

>Old Pratt he is a great musician,
>He spends the summer in hunting and fishin',
>But when the Autumn it does come back,
>He's in the ball room dressed in black.
>CHORUS—Buffalo girls won't you come out to-night?

>Old Pratt he went down to Sandusky Bay,
>He hunted coots eggs every day.
>On web-foot rabbits and spice-foot tea,
>Pratt and old Tear Eye had a spree.
>CHORUS—Buffalo girls won't you come out to-night?

Old Charley, who was with us in camp, evolved the following:

>Andrew hunts with a d—d big gun,
>He shoots his deer while on the run,
>He aims at the heart as they do pass,
>But never brings them to the grass.

Freeport readers who desire to learn more of this song, are referred to the Hon. David H. Sunderland.

There was a multitude of water foul at an early day, but we had little success in hunting them. The modern method of using decoys never occurred to us. Had we used the tactics now in vogue, the bags would have been fabulous. I have no recollection of killing but one goose with a shot gun, although I frequently got them with a rifle. In the spring, the ponds along the Killbuck were fairly black with ducks and geese. Turkeys were plentiful in the timber on the Pecatonica bottoms, but elsewhere in this county were seldom found. Charley Pratt and a Mr. Jackson, also of Freeport, were expert callers and frequently made good bags, but I never got but two; one in the thicket on the site of Thomas Scott's coal yard, the other in the timber above Freeport. Sand hill cranes—quite equal to a turkey—were common, but like the geese, could only be shot with a rifle. The long bill curlew disappeared more than forty years ago. They were here in great numbers up to about 1846, and were excellent for the table. There was a small bird which at that time was called a plover, that came in the spring in countless numbers just before the grass started. They fairly covered the earth where the prairie had recently been burned over, but could only be approached with a team. A few were shot, and we might have made large bags but for the expense of ammunition, a cash article, of which we were deficient. There was no game law at the time of which I write, and it would not have been respected had one been in force. No farmer objected to hunting on his land, neither did we abuse the privilege. We opened the rail fences surrounding large fields when we so desired, and replaced them in good condition. I came to the conclusion long ago, that in a game country, the proper time to shoot it, is when it may be made useful regardless of the season. There is no dish more palatable than a young quail or chicken broiled, when its bones may be eaten with the flesh. We often found early coveys in this condition the first week in August.

In concluding these "REMINISCENCES," I desire to say they are true, and also original except where otherwise stated. Whatever of merit or censure they deserve, belongs to me alone. I have not exhausted the subject by any means, and further, never contemplated writing a history. I was induced to make this attempt as "one of the old guard," and while I write, cannot recall a single individual who was here when I first came, that would be likely to make the attempt. I often found my memory refreshed as the work progressed while consulting with old-timers, all of whom with rare exceptions, willingly gave all the aid in their power. Mr. Edward H. Baker has a mass of matter pertaining to the early history of the county, treating mostly of affairs I have not noticed, which is authentic, and I trust may soon be published. To myself, the most surprising thing in this work, is, that with my training and avocations in life, I should have consented to publish it. I have no apology to offer for the style, and to the critic, will only remark, "where ignorance is bliss," etc.

I am under obligations for information and assistance in divers ways, to the following among others:

To Mrs. Charles H. Spafford and her son Charles H. Spafford, Jr.; Mrs. John H. Sherratt and her sisters, the Misses Wight. The Hon. R. R. Hitt; Miss Mary E. Holmes; Doct. D. S. Clark; Mrs. Harriet Hard of Guilford; Henry N. Baker; Mr. and Mrs. John Lake; Lewis B. Gregory; James B. Howell; S. D. Gregory of Cherry Valley; Edward H. Marsh; Howard D. Frost; James M. Turner; George H. Dennett; Parson K. Johnson of Mankato, Minn.; William H. Tinker of St. Paul, Minn.; Bradford McKenney of Ogle Co.; Edward Mulford; John Nettleton of Los Angeles, Cal.; William A. Manning of Santa Barbara, Cal.; Levi Moulthrop; Ephriam Wyman; Phineas Howes; Charles Waterman and David H. Sunderland of Freeport, Ill.; Mrs. Catherine F. Holland of Cedar Rapids, Iowa; H. H. Robinson; Doct. A. M. Catlin; and to E. A. Kirk. This last old timer—he preceeded me exactly one week—has the most remarkable memory of any whom I encountered while seeking for information, or to confirm or reject some incident brought out, as I was never in a single instance disappointed in my expectations.

JOHN H. THURSTON.

Printed in the USA
CPSIA information can be obtained
at www.ICGtesting.com
LVHW011106241023
761961LV00032B/176